KNOW YOUR NUMBERS

KNOW YOUR NUMBERS

DEMYSTIFYING YOUR
BUSINESS BOOKKEEPING

LESLIE MENARD

ISBN paperback: 978-1-945209-11-6
ISBN ebook: 978-1-945209-12-3

Library of Congress Control Number: 2020950385

Published by Clear Sight Books, Raleigh, North Carolina
Cover by Angie Alaya
Second printing

Contents

Introduction

If you are reading this book, I am going to assume that you are a business owner who has a nagging sense that your understanding of your financial statements is incomplete, that your bookkeeping processes are ad hoc at best, or that the pile of loose receipts and documentation you heave into your CPA's office every year is not an ideal way to approach financial management.

If that's the case, trust me—you are not alone. Unless you are a business owner who has evolved out of an accounting background (like me!), then you probably feel like the process of getting your numbers into order creates an internal reaction that falls on a scale somewhere between mild anxiety and full-on, nausea-inducing stress.

I don't want you throwing up on your keyboard. My goal is to demystify your numbers so you can de-stress! That means:

- helping you understand how to create processes that enable the accurate recording of business transactions,
- teaching you to review and read your financial statements, and
- showing you how to repeat it all, year after year, so you can build a strong, solid business.

We're going to walk through everything in pieces and then pull the whole picture together. If you have a small start-up business or if you have an established business with employees, the structure of bookkeeping is still the same. Those big publicly traded companies use the same basic structure as a sole proprietor—just with bigger numbers and a lot more people to pull it together. Those published financial statements that drive stock prices up and down come from the same kind of transactions you create in your own business.

Know Your Numbers is designed to enhance your knowledge and understanding of the flow of data through your business. Knowing your numbers does not mean you have to know them all off the top of your head. Nor does it mean that you must learn how to do your business bookkeeping. Nope. You've got other, more important and interesting things to fill that part of your brain. But a good business owner understands that there are costs and rewards associated with the inflow and outflow of cash and goods through their business.

Knowing your numbers means that you know how to find, isolate, and identify specific product costs and you know how to summarize sales costs, labor costs, and income (revenue) for various periods.

If you hire a new employee, you need to know the total cost to put them on your payroll. That includes an hourly wage or salary, plus the taxes you pay as an employer.

If you sell retail products, you need to know not only the purchase price of the products, but the costs associated with getting them put on your shelves to sell: delivery, shipping fees, and employee time to unbox, tag with price information, and set up in an attractive display.

Knowing your numbers, again, does *not* mean carrying all of that data around in the front part of your brain—but if you buy a product for $5 per unit and you sell it for $6.50 per unit, you need to know if that $1.50 you are making is enough to cover other costs and still leave a profit. If you have to add $0.25 per unit in shipping and $1.35 in employee time to price, tag, and get the product on your shelf to sell, your actual profit is going to be a negative $0.10 per unit. Knowing the individual total cost of a product is crucial to setting the right selling price.

When you know your numbers, you can work through those smaller calculations that in turn create the bigger calculations. Pricing a combination of products and services gets more complicated, but if you understand how the numbers come together, you can successfully price anything you want to sell—and with confidence. Confidence is good, especially when it's based on good numbers.

As for the actual completion of your bookkeeping work, you might have a bookkeeper on staff, or you might have a contract bookkeeper come in monthly or weekly to help keep your books in order. Or maybe you do all the bookkeeping yourself. No matter what your situation, as the owner of the business, you are responsible for what you report on your tax return, and those numbers flow directly out of the bookkeeping process.

If you begin to understand your business numbers and how they're derived, then you can better monitor those who are working for you. If you don't know what your financial statements are telling you, then how can you know the actual health of your business? If you know how the process works, you can be the backstop that prevents fraud or embezzlement. There are some bad bookkeepers out there, but there are also business owners who turn over the full responsibility of their bookkeeping to someone else. Either or both of those circumstances can spell disaster.

Even if you trust your bookkeeper, that person should not be carrying too much responsibility, have too much access, or function inside your business without any oversight. (Unless your bookkeeper is your spouse or family member—but that's a whole different book.) You should always review their work regularly and even ask for reports randomly. Review who your business is paying, what your business is paying for, and where your income is coming from.

I'm going to do my part to get you more comfortable with the way your data is created and reported, but you need to plan on doing your part too. Your part, for now, includes being willing to look at your business finances and not freaking out.

When you finish this book, you will have new knowledge but also new understanding of where your business numbers come from and how they translate into financial reports. You will have learned to look at your financial reports (without fear!), and you will become more comfortable in translating financial results into business decisions that move you towards your goals.

So let's get into this.

1

Overview

I've been doing bookkeeping work my entire working life in varying levels of scope and responsibility. I started back in the days when you had to record and balance everything by hand. Yeah, no computers. Imagine that! Learning how to record bookkeeping entries into a hand-kept system was a brutal but useful way to learn to balance my work. Here's why . . .

All of accounting is a formula that fits transactions together like a puzzle and is summarized on two financial statements: the Profit & Loss statement and the Balance Sheet. The two of them together tell the full story of your business. The formula itself is made up of all the money flowing in, flowing out, and moving through the business.

Recording transactions by hand and making sure they added up and balanced in the big picture was excellent training for understanding all the nitty-gritty details and how all the little pieces fit together.

You do not need to know everything I know. You do not

need to know everything your certified public accountant or tax professional knows. But understanding *some* of it will give you the confidence and ability to "read" your business finances better.

To demonstrate how the numbers work, I've created a fake company called Doug's Premier Plumbing. We're going to use it throughout the book as an example and a teaching tool. There are a LOT of Doug's Plumbing businesses out there, but this Doug's Plumbing is not real. I created all the financial examples and illustrations for the sole purpose of clarification and demonstration.

I also will refer to QuickBooks Desktop software. There are a lot of other accounting software programs you could be using, and any of them should provide the same information and structure as QuickBooks. Some of the report names might be a little different, but you can use and extract from them the same details I will show you using QuickBooks.

What Do We Mean by Bookkeeping and Accounting?

Let's first get clear on what we mean by bookkeeping and accounting. These are not textbook definitions, but rather the descriptions I use in communicating with clients.

Bookkeeping – The process and function of systematically recording business transactions according to standardized guidelines.

Accounting – The process and function of applying and using skills and knowledge to review, analyze, and interpret bookkeeping data. This might also include making corrections to various entries, restructuring accounts, refining reports to create more clarity, and cleaning up data for optimal tax preparation.

I think you could look at it this way: bookkeeping does the daily work of recording transactions and then is done. Accounting takes the bookkeeping work a step further with analysis and using the numbers for various purposes, such as tax preparation, tax planning, budgeting, or anything else on which future business decisions and actions might be based.

In this book, when I use the term "accounting," that is inclusive of everything in bookkeeping.

Now let's break the definitions down a bit. On any given day in your business, you are creating financial transactions. These transactions can include any of the following:

- Making payments via check, debit card, electronic payment such as ACH or EFT, or other means
- Depositing and recording the receipt of money from sales, a refund from a vendor, a loan draw, or a business owner contribution
- Processing payroll
- Recording a bill as due to be paid at a later date
- Recording a loan payment
- Recording bank charges or bank interest

So basically, anything that generates a financial transaction inside your business is going to be a bookkeeping entry of some kind. Even a monthly deposit of $0.09 bank interest. Yipes. But that's a good thing, right? You want a lot to be going on with your business.

When we define bookkeeping as "systematically recording business transactions," that means doing it the same way every time. If you buy pizza for your office and you record the expenditure to your Employee Recognition account, then next time, don't record it to Travel Meals. Record it to Employee Recognition. The purpose of each transaction should be reflected in how something is recorded so that when you run your reports, the numbers you get are valid—in this case so that you can see how much you are spending on Employee Recognition.

"Systematic" also means recording transactions by the correct date every time; separating transactions by appropriate accounts; and pulling reports by month, quarter, or year. Systems in bookkeeping create the framework for valid reports and credible feedback. Keeping up with bookkeeping every month is critical if you have employees (payroll!), but it also simply keeps you from falling behind.

Say you have your bookkeeper work every week—recording deposits, billing clients, making payments, and generally keeping your books caught up. Then she moves out of state, and you don't replace her right away. You end up managing your cash by what the bank tells you is in your account, and the actual day-to-day bookkeeping activities get set aside. Uh-oh. When you lose continuity in bookkeeping, you also risk losing accuracy.

I've come into businesses where the bookkeeper had been gone for over a year—imagine the mess that had to be cleaned up. Not keeping up can result in lost income (from uninvoiced work), misrecorded payments, or unpaid wage and payroll taxes, not to mention incorrect tax payments (plus the potential for penalties). When data isn't complete and reported, tax agencies may project and assess taxes and penalties based on what they assume your reported earnings would have been.

Being systematic means keeping your bookkeeping current

and consistent. Attach a valid purpose to costs, and then record them appropriately for valid reports later on.

Let's take a simple example: you take four employees to an all-day training conference and buy them lunch between sessions. If you record that meal to Employee Recognition, then you are distorting the total for that account. If you record the lunch meal to Training & Education, then when you run a report, you can see how much you are truly spending on Training & Education (because lunch was part of the day of training, right?).

Now let's carry that same example forward to gain a bit more understanding of the role of accounting in your life. You ask your bookkeeper for month-end financial statements (good for you—look at you go!). When you are reviewing your expenses, your Training & Education total seems like it might be high. You, being the savvy business owner you are, know that you did not have any Training & Education expenses for the previous month. You ask for account detail so you can see what was recorded (or "coded") to that account for the whole year to date.

You find an $85 transaction that stands out as being too low a total for any training and not appropriate to the big picture. When you click into the detail, you see your bookkeeper recorded a large pizza order for the employees to that account. Ah-ha! You can now ask your bookkeeper to recode (or "reclass," which is how we bean-counter types refer to reclassifying transactions) that transaction to Employee Recognition.

Now let's say you ask your bookkeeper for month-end financial statements again, and you look at the numbers. Your sales revenue seems low, so you check the dates on the reports. Your sales total does not include the $5,000 sale made the last day of the month, so you inquire. It turns out your bookkeeper recorded the sale by the invoice date (the date the invoice was created) and not as of the date the work was done, which was the last day of the previous month. Oops. In this simple example, the day the work was performed is generally the date that should go on the invoice. That will record the revenue in the right month.

Dates matter. Dates are part of systematic bookkeeping and accounting, and correcting those transactions to the right date, the right sales account, or the right expense account is part of a good accounting review.

See how that works? Record, review, and then move on to the next month!

Now, just in case you think I am making up rules about being systematic and keeping track of dates, nope! All of these concepts come from a large body of bookkeeping and accounting standards and practices.

Bookkeeping and Accounting Standards and Practices

The standards for bookkeeping and accounting, set many years ago and periodically updated, are called Generally Accepted Accounting Principles, or GAAP (pronounced "gap"). I'll give you a brief history, and I'll keep it brief because you did not buy this book to read an accounting textbook (and I do not want to write one).

Several regulatory agencies and policy boards have developed generally accepted accounting principles over the years as a means of creating consistency and conformity in how companies report their financial data. In the United States, those agencies and boards include the U.S. Securities and Exchange Commission (SEC), the American Institute of Certified Public Accountants (AICPA), the Financial Accounting Standards Board (FASB, pronounced "fazz-bee"), the Governmental Accounting Standards Board (GASB, pronounced "gazz-bee"), and more. Those accounting principles, standards, and procedures are broad rules that have been "adopted by the accounting profession as guides in measuring, recording, and reporting the financial affairs and activities of a business" (*Fundamental Accounting Principles*, Ninth Edition, Pyle & Larson, 1981, p. 11).

Yup, I realize I quoted a textbook that may have been published before you were born! The point is that the information is still relevant. Accounting principles have been in place for many years, and to a great degree, they even cross international borders. I am not going to get into the differences between accounting practices in the United States (where I am located) and the EU or other countries. That's way too complex. What I can address in this book are the basics, but if you are outside the U.S., then you might benefit from following up with an accounting or tax professional in your own country.

Besides sound accounting practices (which we'll address in more detail later), you need consistency (like our earlier pizza example). That simply means you do the same thing the same way each time. The IRS and other tax agencies like to see consistency as well. For example, if your regular practice is to record income when you invoice a client, you cannot suddenly and arbitrarily change tactics. Say you get to the end of a year and your profit is lower than you wanted it to be; you can't record an invoice at year-end for work that is not completed or billable yet just because you want it in by the end of the year. That's a simplified example, but the principle is consistency.

Now let's talk about "good" numbers and why they matter.

Good Numbers

When we talk about the numbers in your business, we are including all the individual transactions, the summaries on reports, the cash flow projections you might work out on a napkin at lunch, and the end-of-cycle financial statements that you hand to banks, lenders, or your CPA. Your business numbers also refer to product costs, payroll costs, and other incremental costs that come together to create a bigger cost.

If you sell gift baskets in various salons and day spas, you need to know the cost of the containers, the lining materials, the products in the basket, and the decorative wrapping. You should also include the cost of your brand packaging, even if it's just a simple tag. Component costs make up a total product cost, and you need to be able to compile them all. And then you add your markup to get the final cost that you present to the salon owners who want to stock and sell your gift baskets.

Your business numbers include all your financial data (it's easier to say "numbers," so I'm going with that, okay?), which encompasses everything from small component costs to the year-end reports used to file tax returns. Those numbers provide critical feedback on the health and well-being of your business. Presumably you want your business to grow, or at least be sustainable, and you need good numbers to make the right decisions to position yourself for growth and stability.

So, what do I mean by "good" numbers? I don't mean huge, happy profits and ideal outcomes. Nope, when I say "good" numbers, I mean accurate, reliable, and valid—even if the numbers look like crap. Even if those numbers say your business is about to fold. Even if those numbers make you want to leap out of your car and land on a barstool.

Good numbers are real.

Good numbers tell the truth.

Good numbers let you know where you stand financially with your business.

You cannot stabilize or grow a business if you make decisions based on invalid data.

You cannot know what to fix inside your business if you don't have the truth.

Does that sound all statistic-y and scary?

Don't be afraid, Muffin! We will work through this. But you have to be willing to see the truth of your business's health. And it just might be far better than you realize.

The basis for creating good numbers in your business is sound bookkeeping practices. That simply means you, or a paid bookkeeper, record your transactions accurately and according to sound practice.

Why Good Numbers Matter

I'm going to give you three straight-up reasons why good bookkeeping numbers matter, okay?

Reason Number 1: Taxes. You file tax returns based on your bookkeeping and accounting numbers. You want to file a return with each tax agency that reports accurate, valid numbers.

Even if you pay more in tax as a result, that means you are making enough money for it to be reportable. This is a good thing!

I know none of us love paying taxes, but it is part of the cost and privilege of owning a business. If you rant and rave about how much the government takes out of your business, you are putting too much energy into anger and negativity. Maybe that sounds woo-woo to some of you, but seriously, running a business is something that most people cannot do. YOU can. You ARE. Please stop being angry about taxes, and celebrate any increase, as it is likely due to an increase in taxable income.

Now, as a quick sidenote, you might benefit from finding a tax professional and talking about ways to reduce your taxable income within your business. It might be time to consider changing entity structures, making an S-Corp election, putting yourself on payroll, or making some other substantive change. Your business is unique and if you want to reduce your taxable income, you need to talk to someone who is a tax pro and can review your situation as it is now. Don't wing this one on your own—there are tax issues that you cannot be expected to know, and consulting with a professional is important.

Reason Number 2: Decision-Making. You must know where your business stands to make good decisions about its development and growth. If you have funky, weird-ass accounting numbers, how can you ever know if the time is right to expand, add a product line, increase staff, or even withdraw some earnings for yourself?

Getting your bookkeeping done right and done consistently is the first step to knowing when and how to develop and grow your business. When you break down your business based on product lines, income streams, or locations, you want to know which are generating the most profit, which are generating the least profit, and which are losing money. You can't fix what you don't know is broken. And you cannot capitalize on strengths if they are hidden inside bogus numbers and inaccurate reports.

Reason Number 3: Selling Your Business. Good numbers give you a basis for setting a price when you decide to sell your business. If you have a business that's providing products and/or services and has a loyal customer base, a strong brand, and proven income, then you have a business worth selling someday.

Your financial statements will create the basis for the selling price. If you own your location (building or land or both), that will certainly factor in, but if you build up your business and can prove its income through financial reports, then you have added to your sales value.

In my experience working with clients, most banks want at least three years of financial statements (Balance Sheet and Profit & Loss) before they will consider a loan to a prospective buyer. You need to start now to build good practices and establish your reportable financial history.

And speaking of reportable financial history, one more important little point: keep your personal and business transactions separate!

Separating Personal and Business Finances

I'm sure that you probably already have separate personal and business banking accounts, but on the odd chance that you have not opened bank accounts solely for your business, I want you to put this book down right now and go do it. And I mean now!

One of the most basic tenets of business ownership is the separation of business and personal funds. I'm going to go out on a limb and say that if you have your business and personal funds all jumbled up in the same bank account, you will not succeed in business long term if you keep operating that way.

Separating your funds doesn't mean you can't draw money out of the business if you own it; it just means that putting personal charges on your business credit card will distort what your business owes. And if you have to go through all your financial data to extract the business expenses, you may miss some, which means paying a higher tax bill than necessary.

If you put business money directly into your personal bank account, the IRS and other tax agencies that have the right to audit your business can look at personal income and bank deposits as potentially taxable. You may be at risk for tax penalties and disallowed business expenses.

Not separating business from personal also looks unprofessional to clients or customers, and, again, to the IRS. The IRS looks at your business as either a "business" or a "hobby." If they deem it a hobby, then you cannot include business expenses as deductions.

I'm simplifying the issue here, but I'm going to say it again: separate your business banking from your personal banking so that you can succeed as a business. It is that important. If you need help, talk to a qualified tax professional or a CPA. I don't care how careful or accurate you are: separating business from personal is foundational to starting and operating a successful business. Period.

Chapter Summary

Bookkeeping and accounting are a vital part of your successful business. Systematically recording business financial transactions gives you feedback on what's working and what's not working inside your business. Systematic bookkeeping means recording transactions the same way each time based on timing and purpose. Systematic bookkeeping also means keeping your books current and valid and organized around date cycles.

"Good" accounting numbers come from good bookkeeping practices and follow generally accepted accounting principles (GAAP). Good numbers tell the truth, and when you have the truth about your business financials, you are in a strong position to initiate changes that create stability and drive growth.

One critical factor in maintaining good business financial data is the separation of personal from business. Not having separate business bank accounts can distort your financial reports, complicate tax issues, and trigger more extensive audits than you might like. Keep all business accounts and transactions separate from your personal accounts and transactions.

2

The Basics of Business Accounting

Before we jump into the ins and outs of financial transactions, I want to review some foundational elements of business. If you are an experienced business owner, you might already be familiar with some of the following, but here's a refresher. And if this is all new to you, don't stress—we're going to sort it out.

Business Structure

Let's talk briefly about how businesses are formed. Your business structure has an impact on the way data is reported and the way you conduct business. I'll review the primary structures here, but if you have any questions about your own business, you need to consult with an attorney or a tax professional.

There are risks and complications associated with each structure, and each can have an impact on your tax return. Do your homework before you commit to one.

The easiest and most basic business structure is a **Sole Proprietorship**. That is simply what you get when one person starts a business. There are very low costs associated, but there are some legal risks. With a sole proprietorship there is no legal separation between the business and the owner, so any business debts or legal claims are going to land on the owner. All the business income flows through and is reported on your annual 1040 tax return.

You can also create a **Partnership**, which is exactly what it sounds like: two or more people conducting business together. The same risks exist as with a sole proprietorship—any business debts or claims affect both partners and their personal assets as well. Federal taxes are not paid on the partnership income as a business, but again, the taxable income flows through to each partner's annual 1040 tax return based on percentage of ownership. The partnership is required to file a return (Form 1065) and possibly several schedules along with it, but any tax due is paid on the partners' personal tax returns.

The next option is a **Limited Liability Company (LLC)**, which formalizes the business structure a bit and offers some legal protection. You can have a single-member LLC or a multiple-member LLC. The LLC structure, whether single- or multiple-member, separates personal assets from business assets. Again, the structure choice depends on your business and the risks each LLC member is going to carry. Income flows through the LLC and is taxed on member/owner tax returns. That's called "pass-through" taxation.

You can also create a **Limited Liability Partnership (LLP)**, which is similar to an LLC or a partnership in that taxation is pass-through, but in some states an LLP can only be formed by licensed professionals such as CPAs, attorneys, and doctors. Some states (e.g., California, Nevada) prohibit licensed professionals from operating as an LLC, but allow formation of a **Professional Limited Liability Company (PLLC)** or an LLP instead. Again, the choice of structure depends on state requirements. With an LLP, one partner is required to be the managing partner and carry the responsibility for the actions of the partnership. The pass-through taxation is based on ownership percentages and partnership agreement terms. Let me be clear about this: partnerships are complicated, especially related to debt, profit distribution, and liability, so make sure you talk to a professional before setting one up.

A **C corporation**, also known as a C-Corp, is probably the most costly business structure to set up, but it creates a business that is taxed on its own. Then the owners (shareholders) are taxed based on dividends paid to them out of the corporation.

An **S corporation**, or S-Corp, is not a company formation structure, but rather an IRS taxation designation, acquired by filing an S-Corp election form with the IRS. I'd recommend doing so only with a tax professional's advice. An S-Corp election can be applied to an LLC or a C-Corp, and it changes nothing but the organization's tax status. The owner of a sole proprietorship or a single-member LLC pays self-employment taxes on business profits, but an S-Corp owner can draw a salary, which gives the business the benefit of the deduction of payroll wages and taxes. Business income still passes through to the business owner(s).

Here's a basic list showing which type of businesses might use which business structure:

- Sole proprietorship: Artist, IT consultant, landscaper, caterer, and other individuals or microbusinesses.
- Single- or multi-member LLC: Any of the sole proprietorships listed above that are going to own assets in the business.
- LLP or PLLC: Professional firms such as doctors, attorneys, and CPAs. This might be determined by state requirements.
- C-Corp: Any business that intends to raise capital by selling stock, carries significant liability risk, or plans to go public at some point.

I want to be clear here: I am only giving you an overview of formation structures, NOT making a recommendation for you and your business. Your situation is unique to you and your tax status. Consult with a professional before you make a structural change in your business. There could be consequences you are not aware of now that could cause significant issues down the road.

What I want you to realize here is that your bookkeeping system will be affected by your business structure. In some cases, it will only result in changes to terminology, but it could also impact reporting and categorizing transactions, as well as affect how your taxes are calculated and paid.

Two Methods of Accounting

Within the structure of accounting, there are two basic methods of recording and reporting your data.

Method 1: Cash. With cash accounting, you record income and expenses only when income is received or when expenses are paid out of your books.

Method 2: Accrual. "Accrual" is a fancy accounting word that means "added in." In this context, it means that you record income when you invoice it, *whether you've received payment or not*, and you record expenses when you know you've incurred them, *not just when they are paid.*

Does accrual seem complicated? It's not really. Think about it this way: if you buy inventory from a vendor and you have 30 days to pay, then you can add the invoice into your books and show it as due in 30 days. You just used the accrual method. If you complete work for a client and invoice them for it, giving them 15 days to pay, you just used the accrual method. All the accrual method does is put income and expenses into the month that each was *created* rather than when it was paid.

Now if you never invoice your customers because they pay you via a cash register in a store, then you are likely on the cash method. And if you pay each bill you owe on the spot, you're using the cash method. That generally works for sole proprietors and smaller businesses, but once you start leveraging time to create more income (buying now and paying when you make the sale), then you need to use the accrual system.

Here's the thing: **you can use only one method**, and, generally speaking, the method you use is determined by how you do business. (Your CPA or tax professional might use a different method for your tax return, but it won't matter to you, so you can let that be off your radar for the moment.)

Set all that aside for now. Go have an adult beverage if the time of day is appropriate and get ready to move on to transactions.

The Chart of Accounts

All of your financial transactions in bookkeeping need to be sorted and categorized before they can be reported.

Think of your bookkeeping like a file cabinet: the cabinet is separated into drawers, and then inside each drawer are hanging folders (you know, those annoying things that hang up sometimes and don't slide out of the way), and inside the hanging folders are single folders. Sometimes there are several single folders grouped together.

Your bookkeeping is a file cabinet of sorts, containing folders sorted according to a standard accounting index.

Remember learning the Dewey Decimal System in school? This is the library system by which books are indexed and placed on shelves. In bookkeeping, your index is called the Chart of Accounts. (See Figure 1 next page.) This is a list of all the "file folders" (accounts) you have available in your business into which you can place "documents" (your transactions).

All bookkeeping transactions are recorded into an appropriate account (file folder) and sorted into date order. The date is critical to the "systematic" part of our bookkeeping definition. It also plays an important role in the validity of your reports.

When the transactions are recorded properly and consistently, your bookkeeping records will sort themselves into the right reports for the right time frame and give you good feedback on your business. Once you understand how each transaction gets to the proper file folder in the right drawer in the file cabinet, you can move on to the big decisions of business ownership.

Chart of Accounts Listing

Account Name	Account Type
1200 · Business Checking	Asset
1202 · Business Savings	Asset
1210 · Accounts Receivable	Asset
1510 · Automobiles & Trucks	Asset
1520 · Computer & Office Equipment	Asset
1540 · Accumulated Depreciation	Asset
2010 · Accounts Payable	Liability
2050 · Credit Card	Liability
2100 · Payroll Liabilities	Liability
2200 · Line of Credit	Liability
2460 · Truck Loan	Liability
3100 · Owner Contributions	Equity
3110 · Owner Draws	Equity
3910 · Retained Earnings	Equity
4110 · Residential Services Income	Income
4120 · Commercial Services Income	Income
5110 · Parts and Materials	Cost of Goods Sold
5200 · Subcontractor Costs	Cost of Goods Sold
6020 · Advertising Expense	Expense
6060 · Bank Service Charges	Expense
6090 · Business License & Fees	Expense
6100 · Car/Truck Expense	Expense
6140 · Charitable Contributions	Expense
6150 · Depreciation Expense	Expense
6160 · Dues and Subscriptions	Expense
6180 · Insurance	Expense
6200 · Interest Expense	Expense
6490 · Office Expenses	Expense
6500 · Payroll Expenses	Expense
6501 · Payroll Wages	Expense
6502 · Payroll Taxes	Expense
6570 · Professional Fees	Expense
6571 · Accounting	Expense
6572 · Legal Fees	Expense
6610 · Postage and Delivery	Expense
6650 · Rent	Expense
6670 · Repairs and Maintenance	Expense
6800 · Telephone	Expense
6900 · Meals and Entertainment	Expense
6970 · Utilities	Expense
7010 · Interest Income	Other Income

Figure 1: Basic Chart of Accounts Listing

Figure 1 shows a sample Chart of Accounts from our fake company, Doug's Premier Plumbing. You will notice account numbers in the far-left column. Accounts can be numbered or not. Numbering can be useful for complex lists of accounts and for creating grouped subaccounts and rolling together related line items, but it is a matter of preference or recommendation by your accountant or bookkeeper. I've used account numbers when a business has a long, complicated list of accounts. A simpler business might not need them.

The Chart of Accounts is organized in a standard order based on the account type each account falls into, and subaccounts are generally shown as indented under a heading account.

The primary categories of accounts include:

- Asset
- Liability
- Equity
- Income
- Cost of Goods Sold (COGS)
- Expense

Let's review each category and what it means.

Asset accounts are things that your business owns: your bank accounts, furniture, equipment, vehicles, inventory you can sell or use in products you sell, and money that is owed to you by customers. We count the money that is owed to you even if it hasn't been paid yet because it will be.

Liability accounts are what you owe to someone else: bills you haven't paid yet (accounts payable), the sales tax you will pay when you file your tax return, loan balances outstanding, and even gift cards/certificates if they have been issued by your business but not yet redeemed.

Equity accounts are your ownership accounts: money you and/or your partners invested to start the business, the money you have contributed throughout the life of the business, and funds you have withdrawn (because, hellooo, that's why you started this thing, right?). Equity accounts are where you will find the business structure reflected.

The way the business owners are referenced changes with business structure as well, as shown in Figure 2.

Business Structure	Owner Reference	Equity Reference
Sole proprietorship	Owner	Owner's equity
Partnership/LLP	Partner	Partners' capital
LLC/PLLC	Member	Members' equity
C Corporation	Shareholder	Common Stock, Treasury Stock

Figure 2: Common Business Structures

Your Chart of Accounts groups each account by category, and each category will determine which financial report the account will show up on. Each category can have subcategories, and those will fall into the right reporting locations as well, assuming each account has been set up properly.

Figure 3 (next page) shows the list of accounts again, this time including the financial statement on which each account appears. Do you see the pattern? All your bookkeeping records are going to fall into this pattern for listing and reporting.

A basic Chart of Accounts will have some standard items on it, but it will also vary with each industry, how you do business, and your business structure. There are too many options to list them all out, but every account will fall into the basic template I've shown you here.

Chart of Accounts Listing		
Account Name	Account Type	Financial Statement
1200 · Business Checking	Asset	Balance Sheet
1202 · Business Savings	Asset	Balance Sheet
1210 · Accounts Receivable	Asset	Balance Sheet
1510 · Automobiles & Trucks	Asset	Balance Sheet
1520 · Computer & Office Equipment	Asset	Balance Sheet
1540 · Accumulated Depreciation	Asset	Balance Sheet
2010 · Accounts Payable	Liability	Balance Sheet
2050 · Credit Card	Liability	Balance Sheet
2100 · Payroll Liabilities	Liability	Balance Sheet
2200 · Line of Credit	Liability	Balance Sheet
2460 · Truck Loan	Liability	Balance Sheet
3100 · Owner Contributions	Equity	Balance Sheet
3110 · Owner Draws	Equity	Balance Sheet
3910 · Retained Earnings	Equity	Balance Sheet
4110 · Residential Services Income	Income	Profit & Loss
4120 · Commercial Services Income	Income	Profit & Loss
5110 · Parts and Materials	Cost of Goods Sold	Profit & Loss
5200 · Subcontractor Costs	Cost of Goods Sold	Profit & Loss
6020 · Advertising Expense	Expense	Profit & Loss
6060 · Bank Service Charges	Expense	Profit & Loss
6090 · Business License & Fees	Expense	Profit & Loss
6100 · Car/Truck Expense	Expense	Profit & Loss
6140 · Charitable Contributions	Expense	Profit & Loss
6150 · Depreciation Expense	Expense	Profit & Loss
6160 · Dues and Subscriptions	Expense	Profit & Loss
6180 · Insurance	Expense	Profit & Loss
6200 · Interest Expense	Expense	Profit & Loss
6490 · Office Expenses	Expense	Profit & Loss
6500 · Payroll Expenses	Expense	Profit & Loss
6501 · Payroll Wages	Expense	Profit & Loss
6502 · Payroll Taxes	Expense	Profit & Loss
6570 · Professional Fees	Expense	Profit & Loss
6571 · Accounting	Expense	Profit & Loss
6572 · Legal Fees	Expense	Profit & Loss
6610 · Postage and Delivery	Expense	Profit & Loss
6650 · Rent	Expense	Profit & Loss
6670 · Repairs and Maintenance	Expense	Profit & Loss
6800 · Telephone	Expense	Profit & Loss
6900 · Meals and Entertainment	Expense	Profit & Loss
6970 · Utilities	Expense	Profit & Loss
7010 · Interest Income	Other Income	Profit & Loss

Figure 3: Chart of Accounts Listing with Financial Statement Location

You can make your Chart of Accounts as complex or as simple as you like. The listing is simply the basis for how you will get feedback from your business transactions. A complex, detailed Chart of Accounts does not necessarily mean a good bookkeeping system. You want to give yourself good information, and sometimes there are other ways to get needed detail.

Think of your Chart of Accounts as a tool for summarizing and grouping transactions, not for providing all the detail.

Transactions

Alrighty, now let's talk more about transactions and how they land in your books. I want you to start thinking in terms of the individual pieces of activity that make up your bookkeeping in general.

Money comes in and money goes out, right? You provide a service; you receive sales revenue. You buy a product; you pay the bill. Sometimes the money goes out like a rock skipping across a pond—that is, a transaction will land a couple of places inside your books before it is completed. For example, you buy printer paper using the business credit card, and then you pay for it when you pay the credit card bill the following month. So the paper is paid for, but it's still an unpaid charge on your credit card until payment is made on the card.

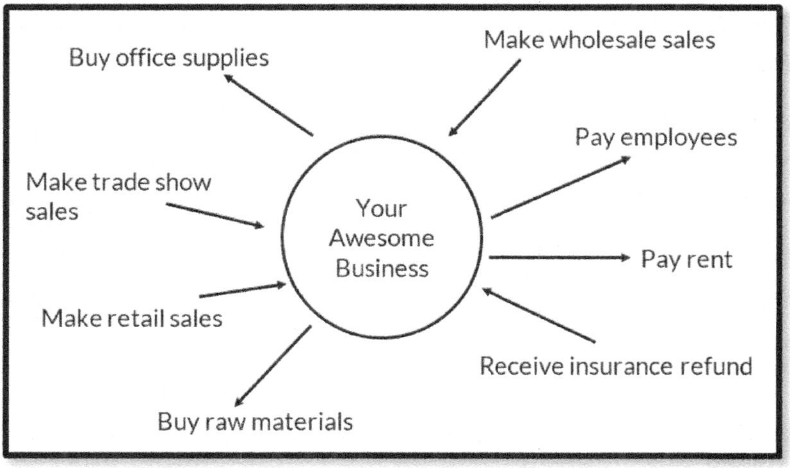

Figure 4: The Flow of Transactions In and Out of Your Business

Daily, depending on the level of activity in your business, you might take in cash payments, check payments, and credit or debit card payments from customers or clients. You might also make a debit or credit purchase, write a check to pay a bill, or write payroll checks to employees.

The various types of transactional activity in your business depend on too many different things to list here. Just remember that you are creating transactions that will go to your bookkeeping system either immediately or in time, and you will see them all later in summary on your reports.

Transaction Dates

Dates are a critical aspect of transactions. The Chart of Accounts will determine which file folder a transaction belongs in, but the date on the transaction will determine which drawer it goes in.

I'll hit this again in later discussions, but just remember that your bookkeeping is organized by date. When your bank asks for financial statements, you will want to make sure that you print a Balance Sheet with the right month-end date. You also want to print a Profit & Loss statement that covers the same period and ends on the same date as the Balance Sheet. This gives someone a complete financial snapshot of your business. If your dates don't match, then the numbers won't line up and make sense.

One other note here: when you print financial statements, you generally want to print them as of the last month-end date they were reconciled. That bit is important. If you have an appointment at the bank on July 18 and you take in financial statements dated July 17, they are going to wonder if your numbers are current and valid and why you picked an odd date. If, however, you give them statements with a month-end date of June 30, it's immediately apparent that you have a good handle on your bookkeeping, that you've finished and reconciled your books through the end of the previous month, and that July is still a work in progress.

Now, back to transactions. Each transaction you generate in your business has a date that sorts it into the right financial drawer. Invoices you send to your customers have an invoice date and payment terms that set a due date (when the customer should pay by). Bills that you owe have a bill date, and when you record a bill by that date, it goes into your books as what you owed as of that date. So a water bill that has a bill date of June 30 will be recorded as a June expense, and the due date, which could be July 15, has no accounting impact other than as a reminder when you should pay it. Check dates, payroll pay dates, deposit dates, and on and on. All of those transactions are automatically sorted and filed by the date on them.

Now the other aspect of transaction dates is that when you record transactions by the right date, you can tell if you made money or lost money that month, spent more than you sold on inventory, or paid the rent twice in the same month. So if you pay the July rent on July 1, and then pay the August rent on July 31, don't date the check July 31; date it August 1. That way you control the drawer each rent transaction lands in, and you sort them by month.

When you are aware of dates, you have a stronger grasp of the flow of money through your business. It flows in by date, and it flows out by date. Recording each transaction by the correct date gives you a consistent format for your reports. And it means you have a better idea of what's really happening inside your business. Using the rent example again, if rent checks for both July and August are dated in July, your financial reports will show double rent in July and no rent in August. When you look at the bottom line, your profit is going to reflect that as well. Or, if you have a retail business that is heavily seasonal, you want to know how that increased income will flow in, because there will most certainly be increased expenses to flow out as well.

Double-Entry Bookkeeping

Each financial transaction you record always affects two or more accounts. Always.

Sit down (if you aren't already) and take a deep breath.

Today's bookkeeping is called "double-entry accounting." Every account has an "in" side and an "out" side (money goes in or out). And each transaction has two sides (money going out of one account and into another), so each transaction will always affect two (or more) accounts. Double-entry accounting means that every entry to an account requires an offsetting entry to one or more other accounts. There. That simple. Double-entry accounting.

But what does double-entry accounting look like in real life? Truthfully, with accounting software, it is partially hidden from view, but I want you to understand what goes on in the background.

Think of a bookkeeping transaction as having an **action** and a **definition**. I tell my clients "Do the thing, and then explain it." You write a check (action: take money out of the bank account), and you tell your bookkeeping software what it was for (define it: for rent). The check writing is the first half of the process; telling your software what the check was for, or giving it a business purpose, is the second half. Your "double-entry" in this case means you will record an "out" to the bank account and an "in" to the Rent Expense account.

If you receive money from a customer and deposit it to your bank account, the deposit is the action and the definition is "sales." But if you make a bank deposit and don't tell your bookkeeper what it was for, there is no definition to the entry. The action is the deposit, but there's no definition there. What was the check for? Was it for a product sale? Was it a refund on liability insurance? Was it a refund from a vendor for a product return? There must be a valid definition to attach to an action.

Remember how you used to write checks (maybe you still do)? In your check register you recorded checks out and bank deposits in using two different columns. Now remember we said every account in your business has two sides: an In and an Out. Every single account in your Chart of Accounts (except for one special account that we'll talk about later) has a register associated with it—just like your old checkbook.

And you can draw out every transaction using what we call "T-accounts"—like the separate columns in your bank register.

Using the payment of rent as an example, it looks like this:

Checking		Rent Expense	
	$1,000.00	$1,000.00	

Figure 5: T-Account for Rent Payment

You see a T-account for Checking with $1,000, and a T-account for Rent Expense with $1,000—but how do you know if money is going in or out of each account? The location of the money on one side of the T or the other indicates whether it is going In or Out of that account.

In this case the $1,000 on the right side of the Checking T-account is money going Out; that is, the account is decreasing. The $1,000 on the left side of the Rent Expense T-account is coming In; that is, the account is increasing.

So, action = payment made and definition = rent. And both sides—Out of Checking and In to Rent Expense—match amounts. Your rent payment represents cash out of your checking account and an increase to your rent expense.

We use the terms "debit" and "credit" to explain which side of the T-account increased or decreased. And this is where we vary from the check register analogy. Outside of accounting we tend to think of "credit" as meaning your account is getting something, and we think of "debit" as meaning something is coming out of your account.

Let that go.

When we are talking about bookkeeping and accounting, debit means "left" and credit means "right."

Yikes. Really?

Yes.

Now, the part that gets complicated is that different categories or types of accounts increase or decrease on different sides. Asset accounts increase on the debit (left) side. Liability and Equity accounts increase on the credit (right) side. Don't get too hung up on this part—you can accept it as fact and just move past it. Your bookkeeper is the one who needs to get it.

This is where a lot of "bookkeepers" (I'm using quotes here because not everyone who calls themselves a bookkeeper is qualified to do so) go wrong.

Without understanding which accounts increase on which side, today's bookkeeping software systems will force both sides to match. Sometimes the default works, and sometimes it creates problems. When one of my clients writes a check and is not sure which account(s) the payment definitions should land in, I tell them to use an account called Ask My Accountant. Or an account called Suspense. That puts any confusing transactions into a single place for me to look, and it makes corrections easier.

I'm throwing a lot at you, but you're doing great! I'm going to talk a bit more about double-entry accounting, but that's because I want you to understand that each financial action in your business MUST also have a definition.

Let's list out a few two-sided transactions in Figure 6 so you can see the pattern.

Transaction Intention	Action (Account)	Definition (Account)
Pay the rent via check	Record the check as a decrease to Checking	Record an increase to Rent Expense
Deposit an insurance refund check	Record the deposit as an increase in Checking	Record a decrease to Insurance Expense
Buy merchandise to sell	Record a bill due as an increase to Accounts Payable	Record an increase to Inventory
Pay the electricity	Record an online bill payment as a decrease in Checking	Record an increase to Utilities Expense
Order display shelves	Record a bill due as an increase to Accounts Payable	Record an increase to Display Expense
Buy cleaning supplies from Costco	Record the check as a decrease to Checking	Record an increase to Janitorial Expense

Figure 6: Transaction Actions and Definitions by Account

See how that works?

Now, what if a transaction has more than one definition? We'll use one example: Costco. Let's say you used your debit card there and (because no one buys just a single item at Costco) it came to a total of $238.56. You bought a tub of red vines, muffins, printer paper, a chair mat, and a whole bunch of cleaning supplies. You are going to record the debit purchase out of your checking account, but then you are going to split the definition by however many accounts it takes to define what you bought. Just remember that your definition accounts must add up to the same amount as the debit purchase.

Transaction Intention	Action (Account)	Definition (Accounts)
Purchase cleaning and office supplies at Costco	Record debit card payment as a decrease in checking	Record increases to Janitorial Expense, Office Supplies, and Employee Meals

Figure 7: Transaction Action Account with Multiple Definition Accounts

There! It's that simple. There are certainly more complicated entries in the world of business, but in principle it's simple. Just remember: transaction = action + definition.

Chapter Summary

Business bookkeeping is a systematic way of recording financial transactions.

The business structure you choose for your business—sole proprietor, partnership, corporation—has an effect on your bookkeeping and accounting, so be sure to get proper legal and tax advice in setting up your business.

Bookkeeping systems can be kept in one of two ways: cash or accrual. With cash accounting, you record income and expenses only when income is received or when expenses are paid out of your books. With accrual accounting, you record income when you invoice it (regardless of whether you've been paid), and you record expenses when you know you incur them (not just when they are paid).

Your bookkeeping transactions are organized by the Chart of Accounts, which is essentially your list of accounts (your accounting "file folders"), and by date (your "file cabinet drawers"). A standard accounting system uses categories of accounts—asset, liability, equity, expense, cost of goods sold, and income—which automatically sort out to the appropriate report, such as the Profit & Loss statement or the Balance Sheet.

Double-entry bookkeeping means every transaction has two sides—an action and a definition—and it will always affect a minimum of two accounts. Both sides of a transaction must add up to the same amount.

Always use the right dates and the right accounts as you record your transactions. That is the foundation for good financial feedback.

3

How Common Transactions Work

Now that you understand the basics of business transactions, let's work through some of the common ones you will create in your business. Most transactions happen with ease and without much notice. Not a lot of deep thought goes into them. They happen simply because you conduct business. In any given day you might order products to sell, pick up a latte for your receptionist (No? Well, it would be a nice thing to do.), use online banking to pay your utility bill, upload hours worked to your payroll provider, or ring up sales through a point-of-sale (POS) system.

Each one of those actions creates a bookkeeping entry that, in one way or another, needs to be recorded. You might have a point-of-sale system that is linked to your bookkeeping software, or you might be using a payroll provider like ADP,

Paychex, or QuickBooks to process your payroll. Sometimes those systems will create the entry for you, but sometimes you have to do it yourself.

We will walk through some of those basic transactions and the possible bookkeeping entry that each creates. I cannot cover all the possibilities here (no one wants to read THAT book), but I'll hit some of the common ones.

One other thing I want to say here is that bank feeds have radically simplified the process of recording transactions. Bank feeds are data buckets in which your bank or credit card activity can sit until you actively route the transactions into your bookkeeping software. The bank feed is helpful, but each transaction is coming from the bank or credit card provider and will not have all the necessary bookkeeping information attached to it. And with cloud-based accounting tools, such as QuickBooks Online and Xero, the transactions flow in almost automatically in real time, making it easy to overlook the missing information.

Let me say that again: your accounting bank feed is incomplete until you fill in the rest of the blanks!

So, for example, if you use checks, in the Payee field, you must enter the name of the payee before you import the transaction into your bookkeeping. I've seen a LOT of cloud-based systems go so very wrong because the owner did not record to whom the payment was made. If you import the feed without that information, you get a bunch of expenditures recorded to accounts with no ability to determine who they went to.

Before importing your bank feed transactions into your accounting system, you can edit and then add or match your transactions. If you use your debit card frequently, be sure to add the payee when you review your bank feed. If you use cloud accounting such as Xero or QuickBooks Online, you will make your business life much easier by recording checks *first* and then matching them from the bank feed. The more you can match, the more complete your books will be. Trust me: adding the details to transactions from the beginning will make the rest of your bookkeeping and accounting much easier.

And one more note for U.S. businesses: you must issue a 1099 at the end of the year to any non-employee to whom you have paid $600 or more that year for rent, services, or legal fees. If you do not add a payee (for example, for your rent checks) you will not be able to issue a 1099 because when you look up your landlord's vendor file, there will be nothing there. Enter the names so you can file those transactions appropriately!

Speaking of rent and other payments, let's look at paying bills and how those transactions are created and recorded (entered) in your bookkeeping. And since we left off with a rent example, we'll go there first.

Basic Payment

You likely pay your rent via check or by making an online bank payment. This is one of the most straightforward business transactions you can make. I mean, you want to keep your business open, so you remember to pay your rent every month without receiving a bill or notice, right?

When recording this transaction, one thing to consider is whether or not any other costs are included in your rent. Sometimes a commercial lease agreement will be a "triple net" lease. That means in addition to your rent, you are paying your net share of three fees: property taxes, building insurance, and common area maintenance. You can write the payment into your bookkeeping and define it all as Rent Expense, or you can bust it all out into four separate expenses (rent, taxes, insurance, maintenance).

Why would you use four accounts if one account works?

Well, if your lease agreement allows for adjusting costs as they increase throughout the year, your financial statements will show specifically what increased, rather than burying it in Rent Expense. So, for example, you'll know whether your rent went up due to an insurance increase or some other factor.

The other reason to separate these accounts is so that you have a better basis for comparison if you decide to consider moving. If one of the new locations you are considering does not offer a triple net lease, you can still easily compare rent to rent if you've separated the actual rent expense on your books. Most accounting systems let you save repeat transactions, which means you only have to enter the four-way split one time and then let your software do the entry every time after that. You can also tell your software to "memorize" transactions. That means when a repeat payment comes up, the entry portion is remembered, saved, and done for you. So if you want this level of detail, it is not difficult to capture. Sweet!

Paying rent or paying for something else you don't receive a bill for is easy—you just make and record the payment. I recommend that you use the check number field to write out the manner of payment, even if it was not a numbered paper check. For example, "Debit," "ACH," or "EFT" will all fit in that field in most software systems. I also sometimes use "auto" to signify a payment that was made via a previously agreed-upon automated deduction.

Here is how your rent payment lands in your books:

- Accounts affected: Increase to Rent Expense, decrease to Cash/Checking
- Reports affected: Profit & Loss for Rent Expense, Balance Sheet for Cash/Checking

Bill Entry for Later Payment

The other way to make payments is to schedule them via Accounts Payable. Accounts Payable is a holding tank in which you record bills that you are not yet ready to pay. This gives your books a record of the expense, but instead of deducting it from your Cash (bank) account, it records to Accounts Payable. It only affects Cash when the payment is actually made.

Let's use a two-sided entry for the purchase of inventory and supplies from the same vendor: you record the action as a bill that is due in 30 days, which increases Accounts Payable. Then your definition on the "enter a bill" screen is the split between the expense accounts that apply, such as Inventory and Office Supplies.

When the bill becomes due and you are ready to make a payment, you are going to reduce Accounts Payable and you are going to reduce your Cash/Checking account. There's no entry to the expense accounts because you already made that entry when you recorded the bill as due.

Here's what it looks like in two separate transactions:

ENTRY 1: SCHEDULE BILL

- Accounts affected: Increase to Inventory, increase to Supplies Expense, increase to Accounts Payable
- Reports affected: Balance Sheet for Inventory and Accounts Payable, Profit & Loss for Supplies Expense

ENTRY 2: PAY BILL

- Accounts affected: Decrease to Accounts Payable, decrease to Cash/Checking
- Reports: Balance Sheet for both again

Debit Card Payment

A debit transaction represents cash out of your account almost immediately. If you stop on the way to work and pick up coffee and doughnuts for your employees, the odds are good that by the time you get to work, the charge has been deducted from your bank account.

If you use bank feeds (especially for cloud-based accounting), as we talked about earlier, you are simply going to make sure the transaction is posting to the correct account (file folder!) from your bank feed. Simple, right?

If you do not sync your bookkeeping to your bank accounts, then you will have to enter the transaction manually. In QuickBooks, you would either open your bank register or go to the "write checks" function. In the check number field, enter "debit" or leave it blank, enter the name of the business you paid (Sweet Spot Donuts & Coffee), and the amount. Pick an appropriate account (such as Employee Recognition), and save the transaction.

ENTRY: DEBIT CARD PURCHASE

- Accounts affected: Increase to Employee Recognition, decrease to Cash/Checking
- Reports affected: Profit & Loss for Employee Recognition, Balance Sheet for Cash/Checking

PRO TIP: Don't rely on your bank balance to tell you what's available to spend. I've seen too many business owners lose track of their bank balances consistently and rapidly because they used their debit card for everything. The bank is simply reporting and showing you what has already cleared. If you have other payments that are issued but have not cleared the bank, then your bank balance is lying to you. When you keep your bookkeeping current, you know more about what's going on than the bank does. That puts you in control, and you're not just passively allowing the bank to tell you what's going on.

I'm not saying to ignore your online bank balance. I'm just telling you that to be in control of your business, your money, and your strategy, you must own it from the front lines—that is, from your accounting system, which should always have more information than your online banking. If you look at your bank charges and see you are paying several NSF (non-sufficient funds) charges or overdraft fees per year, then I'm telling you that you are not in control. Everyone can make a mistake and overdraw a bank account. If you are doing it regularly, then you are not correctly managing your bookkeeping or your funds.

That's enough on debit charges, so let's move on to credit card transactions.

Business Credit Card Charge

If you use credit cards, ideally you have one dedicated for business use only—just like you keep banking accounts separate, it's best to keep credit accounts separate. However, that's not always what happens, so in this section we'll start with the recording and processing of dedicated business credit card charges, and then in the next section we'll talk about how to record a business payment made using a personal credit card.

If you use cloud accounting and your business credit card account is linked, then any charges you make will roll into your bank feed. You will need to review each one and either match it or add it—just like you did with your checks. As always, be sure to choose the correct definition account. If you are using desktop accounting software, you can either download all the charges from your bank or enter them yourself.

Whether using a bank feed or entering your credit card charges one at a time, you still have not paid the credit card bill yet. All the transactions are still sitting inside your business, both as expenses and as a balance owed on your credit card.

When you make a payment on the credit card, there are two ways to record the payment: a full payment on the balance, or a partial payment with a balance you carry forward. Either way, you record a payment (check or EFT) to the Credit Card liability account as your definition account. That will decrease the credit card balance.

So here's what the two transactions look like on your books:

ENTRY 1: CHARGE ON CREDIT CARD

- Accounts affected: Increase to Office Supplies, increase to the Credit Card liability account
- Reports affected: Profit & Loss for Office Supplies expense, and Balance Sheet for Credit Card

ENTRY 2: MAKE PAYMENT ON CREDIT CARD

- Accounts affected: Decrease to Credit Card liability account, decrease to Cash/Checking
- Reports affected: Balance Sheet for both

Personal Credit Card Charge

Now for many small businesses (such as my own), there is not a compelling need for a dedicated business credit card, so occasionally business expenses are put on a personal credit card.

For example, as the owner of Doug's Premier Plumbing, while you're buying groceries (and God knows what else) at Costco, you come across a good price on some awesome tool you think you need for your business. So you add it to the pile in the cart and move on to the outdoor furniture . . . Fade to the cash register: Uh-oh, no business debit or credit card with you. Oh well. You pay for your Costco purchases with your personal credit card and head for the car.

How do you get that expense into your business bookkeeping? And why does it matter?

Option 1: Expense Reimbursement. If you use your personal credit or debit card only occasionally for business expenses, then you can reimburse yourself.

The easiest way to do that is to write up an expense report (there are tons of examples online) and either withdraw, transfer, or pay yourself back for that specific amount. Attach your receipts to the expense report, and file it like you would any other business receipt.

But that's not a sound practice to use all the time, so if you make regular business purchases on your personal cards, you really do need a dedicated business debit or credit card.

Option 2: Owner Contribution. The second option is to record the business transaction as an owner contribution to the business. Say what? Let's back up a bit.

As a business owner, you draw money out of your business and sometimes you put money into it. When you put money in, it's called an owner contribution, and it increases your Equity account. When you take money out it's called an owner's draw, and it decreases your Equity account. Instead of getting an expense reimbursement, you can consider the amount you spend on your personal debit or credit card a "contribution" to the business.

I'll give you the basics of entering an owner's contribution transaction, but you may want to ask a qualified bookkeeper to give you some assistance since software packages vary on how this is accomplished.

- Go to the menu option for creating a Journal Entry.
- Remember you are doing an action and a definition. Your action is going on the first line: Owner Contributions (or a similar name) will be the first account.
- Enter the amount of the business purchase made out of your personal funds as a Credit, and put in a decent description (e.g., "bought adjustable pipe wrench with a personal credit card at Costco").
- On the second line, put in the definition part of the transaction: Small Tools Expense is the account, and make sure the same description from the first line fills in on the second line (it should be automatic).

Figure 8 (next page) provides a screenshot from QuickBooks to show how that journal entry would look.

PRO TIP: If you use a personal credit card for business expenses, do not add the credit card to your business accounting system. If you create an account for your personal credit card and only record business transactions to it, there is no way to reconcile it (see more about reconciliations in Chapter 7). Since there is no way to officially validate the balance, the transactions end up hanging out in space, so to speak.

Figure 8: Journal Entry Screenshot of Owner Contribution

SPECIAL NOTE: A journal entry is generally something a bookkeeper does to adjust and correct something that cannot be done any other way, so I'm going to discourage you from making entries to your books this way. Without the understanding that comes from accounting training and experience, a journal entry can go sideways fast. I've given you the bones of what to do, but making a journal entry to record transactions for items paid out of your personal funds should be rare. I highly recommend you save those receipts and give them to your bookkeeper at the end of the month. They can do a single journal entry for everything you contributed to your business from your personal funds.

The important point is that you realize there are multiple ways of creating accounting entries for your business. You should always choose the way that is the most appropriate for the type of transaction you are entering. (More on that later.)

Why am I hammering on getting this type of credit card transaction right? Remember that you as a person are separate from the business you are operating, and that your business financial statements tell the story of your business. You will pay taxes on the bottom line, and someday you may want to show a prospective buyer that you properly and accurately recorded all the costs of the business and that the asking price is valid!

Make sense? Separation of business and personal is important, but if you do create a crisscross, be sure to pull the transactions out and separate them appropriately.

Sales

Oh yeah, here's the good stuff: sales. This is why you're in business, right?

There are two basic ways to record sales and income from sales: on the spot through the actual receipt of payment, or via an invoice for which you will receive payment later. The system you use will depend on how your business makes sales.

If you have a cash register (fixed in a store) or a point-of-sale (POS) system on a tablet or your phone (good for mobile sales), you record sales when you receive money—all in one transaction.

If you perform work and then send the customer an invoice after the work is complete or at the end of the month, then you are recording a sale and making a separate transaction when you receive the money—two transactions.

Let's look at the bookkeeping entries for each option.

Option 1: Receive Money Immediately. First, let's review the kind of transaction where you receive money at the same time you make the sale. That could be from a fixed cash register system in your store or, like Doug's Premier Plumbing, you might use a phone or tablet to swipe a credit card on the client jobsite. However you receive money in your business, you are creating an entry for the sale of a product or service with an offsetting deposit.

If you make cash sales all day, you are probably going to do one big bank deposit and make one sales record for the day. If you use a phone or tablet app, you probably record individual sales.

Either way, the effects of the transactions are the same:

- Accounts affected: Increase to Sales, increase to the Sales Tax Payable liability account (only if applicable; don't panic—I'm going to address sales tax next!), increase to Cash
- Reports affected: Balance Sheet for Cash/Bank account and Sales Tax Payable, Profit & Loss for Sales

Option 2: Invoice for Later Payment. Now let's look at when you complete work or make a sale and then invoice the customer after the fact or at the end of the month.

In this case, your invoice records the sale at the time you create the invoice. That increases Sales and it also increases Accounts Receivable. Then when you receive the payment from the customer (either in part for a deposit or in full for the whole balance), you record the payment against the Accounts Receivable record.

A common mistake is to record the deposit as a sale again; that actually doubles the entries to Sales and leaves the Accounts Receivable invoice open and showing as unpaid. Big oops. Don't do that—it will not give you good sales numbers!

The effect of recording a sale from an invoice means you are recording income without receiving the cash. This kind of system needs a little bit more tracking to keep it accurate and current.

Here's the effect of creating an invoice and receiving payment later:

ENTRY 1: CREATE INVOICE

- Accounts affected: Increase to Sales, increase to Accounts Receivable
- Reports affected: Profit & Loss for Sales, Balance Sheet for Accounts Receivable

ENTRY 2: RECEIVE PAYMENT

- Accounts affected: Decrease to Accounts Receivable, increase to Cash
- Reports affected: Balance Sheet for both

Remember our discussion of accounting systems—cash versus accrual? Well, this sales thing is how it looks in action. When you make sales and collect/deposit payment at the same time, you are using the cash system. That's how you will report your business results.

When you create invoices and wait for payment, your accounting system is accrual. There's nothing wrong with either system—just know there are differences, and make sure you or your bookkeeper will be generating reports with the right setting.

Sales Tax and Use Tax

Okay, let's talk a little bit about sales tax and other taxes you pass on to your clients or that you yourself will owe. This stuff is not fun—I get that. However, if you don't keep up with this part, you will either cripple your business or go out of business. I'm serious.

Depending on where your business is located, you may have several different tax agencies to report to with several different tax rates, but for the sake of simplicity here, I'm going to use a single sales tax rate.

I'm in the state of Washington, where the state's Department of Revenue tracks and collects sales tax for counties and cities and provides a combined state and local tax rate so that business owners do not need to track local rates separately. Many other states do the same thing, but you will need to check your own state or governmental agencies to find out what your tax reporting requirements are.

When you ring up or make a taxable sale, you record the sale, add the sales tax, and charge the customer the full amount. They pay you for your product, and they pay you for the sales tax. You are collecting both amounts, but only one of them is yours. Don't forget this part: the sales tax you collect is NOT your money.

Let's use the sale of a $100 item with 8.5% sales tax as an example in Figure 9. A total of $108.50 is collected.

Product sales	$ 100.00
Sales tax 8.5%	$ 8.50
Total collected	$ 108.50

Figure 9: Sample Sales Tax Calculation

So how much of that is yours? Only $100.00. Here's my best suggestion for handling sales tax: use a separate bank account. Depending on how your sales are handled, you could either split the daily deposit between two bank accounts, or you could transfer the sales tax total once a week.

Either way, I strongly suggest that you never, ever think of the total amount collected as "yours." Pull the tax out and set it aside. If your POS system is set up properly, then the sales tax is being recorded on your Balance Sheet as a liability. You collected it, and you owe it. No one is taking anything away from you. Without the sales tax, your sale would still only be $100.00 in this example.

If you collect the money and spend it without remitting it to the tax agency when it's due, you are digging a very deep hole for your business to fall into. And if you rely on future sales to cover your previous tax liability, then you are spending current revenue on prior debt. That's a treadmill that will escalate in speed and eventually come to a sudden stop with sad results.

Based on my experience with clients, when you say, "I don't owe that tax until next month," you really should already have the money set aside in a separate bank account to cover it. Then when you say you don't owe it yet, you can also say "but I've set aside the funds to cover it!" Then you do a happy dance because you are a freaking awesome business owner.

Let's cover one additional issue here that's related to sales tax: use tax. Use tax is a self-applied sales tax. You will owe it any time you buy an item wholesale or without paying sales tax, and you end up using (not reselling) that item in your business.

Here's a Doug's Premier Plumbing example: Doug buys plumbing supplies and materials from vendors. When he makes a purchase, there is no sales tax applied because the vendors are set up to sell to Doug wholesale. When Doug then uses the supplies for his customers, he charges them retail prices and charges/collects sales tax.

One day the bathroom sink in Doug's office springs a leak. He doesn't have to call anyone because he's got in-house skills to fix it! He pulls the parts and supplies out of inventory and makes the repair. However, recall that Doug has not paid sales tax on the parts. Since he has now used the parts and they are no longer available to sell to customers, he owes what's called "use tax" on the parts.

Use tax is basically the same as sales tax, just accounted for separately, and it is often submitted along with sales tax on a monthly or quarterly basis. Each state is different, so I'm not going to go into more detail here; you'll need to look at the requirements that apply to your business.

What I want you to take away is that use tax can and should accrue (add up) the same way sales tax does, and you can be audited by tax agencies for your use-tax accounting. You should record and pay it as required, and you can handle it the same way you do sales tax.

Payroll and Payroll Taxes

Payroll is complicated. I'm not going to pretend it isn't. If you have employees on payroll and you hate doing your bookkeeping, then you will reduce your stress and your long-term costs, and increase your peace of mind, by hiring a bookkeeper, paying for a service, or getting some form of skilled assistance.

There are likely more legalities associated with payroll than any other aspect of your accounting. When you commit to paying people to perform work on your behalf, you are creating a contract with multiple tax agencies, your employees, and the government. You must adhere to the laws and statutes that surround the process and act of paying employees. Period.

In short, the process of payroll requires consistent, regular pay periods. The requirements are too extensive to address here, so I will just cover the basic and most critical transactions.

When you create a paycheck for an employee, you withhold their share of any taxes. In the U.S. that's Social Security, Medicare, and federal income tax. It may also mean a state income tax and a portion of the cost of worker's compensation, which is an insurance to cover injuries sustained on the job.

When you withhold taxes from an employee's check, you have a legal, moral, and ethical obligation to remit those taxes on the employee's behalf. You, as the employer, also owe your share of taxes that are generated by the process of paying that employee. Again, I strongly suggest a separate bank account to segregate funds for these taxes. Transfer an amount into the payroll tax bank account that is the equivalent of what you owe. Do not freakin' spend it!

I'm going to say that again. If you run payroll and deduct a total of $1,000 from your employees' checks, do not pay your bills with it. Do not transfer it to your personal account to make your car payment. Hold that money in an appropriately segregated bank account until you are required to pay it.

Payroll transactions affect several accounts in a couple of entries: the first when the paychecks are paid out, and the second when the payroll taxes are paid.

ENTRY 1: WRITE PAYCHECKS

- Accounts affected: Increase to Wages Expense, increase to Payroll Tax Expense (employer share), and increase to Payroll Taxes Payable (combined employer and employee taxes not yet paid)
- Reports affected: Profit & Loss for expenses, Balance Sheet for Payroll Taxes Payable

ENTRY 2: PAY PAYROLL TAX

- Accounts affected: Decrease to Payroll Taxes Payable, decrease to Cash
- Reports affected: Balance Sheet for both

Documentation and Support for Transactions

Transactions are the ultimate content in your business accounting. As such, they need to be supported by receipts and documentation that validate their role in the business.

Yes, I know some of you feel that keeping receipts is archaic and too old-school for you. Okay, but . . . the Internal Revenue Service and other tax agencies use those receipts to validate your tax returns, your filed reports, and the claims of business expenses. Whether you keep paper or electronic copies, they need to be kept.

I suggest that you set up an electronic filing system that matches your physical filing system. Back it up regularly to the cloud or to an external hard drive. Whatever works for you is fine—just back it up.

I have a client who says he gets all his invoices emailed to him, and he doesn't print them out. I asked him how he would handle an audit, and he said he'd log into his account with each supplier and print out the invoices. So I asked what he would do if the supplier went out of business before the audit.

I'm all for saving paper, but I would encourage you to NOT expect your suppliers, utility providers, and anyone else you pay to store your records for you. Download and save your copies.

Recently I helped a client with a partial audit by a state tax agency. When he could not produce a receipt that showed a tax had been paid, the assumption was made that it had *not* been paid. He ended up owing back taxes as well as penalties and interest. It was not fun or pretty, but it could have been much worse.

One other aspect of keeping business documents is the retention period—that is, how long you have to store that stuff before you can get rid of it.

Each state has different laws, as does the Internal Revenue Service. When you get to the end of your fiscal year, box your records up, label it with the contents and the year, and secure it. Search out "retention requirements" by state agency and on the IRS website, and then keep the boxes for as long as the longest required period.

If you ever have to pull something out, having your boxes labeled—in detail—will save your sanity. You might think that you'll remember you filed your reconciled bank statements with your payroll reports and records, but—and trust me on this—after a year or more, that memory track has been overwritten with more interesting and important data. List your box contents, add the year it represents, and forget it until you need it.

Chapter Summary

Every financial transaction in your business has an impact on your financial statements. There's an action and a definition associated with each—and sometimes more than one definition. Transactions can be split into as many definitions as you like to give you the kind of information you want on your financial statements.

When a transaction, or a series of transactions, creates a liability for which you will need to later remit payment, set the funds aside in a separate bank account. That might include payroll taxes, sales tax, or use tax. Knowing you have the funds to cover what you owe when you owe it will reduce your stress. Remember that tax withheld from employee checks and sales tax collected from customers is not your money.

All your business transactions need to be supported by documentation. Store your records in either paper or electronic form. Don't leave them in your email or in an account with a supplier. Sometimes businesses are sold or closed, and that could mean their records disappear, so keep your own.

4

Decoding Financial Statements

Once you have "filed" your business transactions correctly using the appropriate accounts and dates, you can then get summarized information about all of it by telling your accounting software (or your bookkeeper) to print you a report.

We've briefly mentioned your financial statements in previous sections, but now we're going to talk about how the results from all your business activity transactions land on your financial statements. There are two primary reports we are going to talk about: your Profit & Loss statement, often abbreviated P&L, and your Balance Sheet.

On the next two pages, using our fake plumbing company as an example, you'll see what a Balance Sheet and a P&L statement look like. (Don't be intimidated by them—keep reading!)

Doug's Premier Plumbing, Inc.
Balance Sheet
As of October 31, 2018

	Oct 31, 2018
ASSETS	
Current Assets	
Checking/Savings	
Business Checking	35,457.19
Business Savings	500.00
Total Checking/Savings	35,957.19
Accounts Receivable	
Accounts Receivable	8,125.00
Total Accounts Receivable	8,125.00
Total Current Assets	44,082.19
Fixed Assets	
Computer & Office Equipment	2,500.00
Accumulated Depreciation	-846.12
Total Fixed Assets	1,653.88
TOTAL ASSETS	45,736.07
LIABILITIES & EQUITY	
Liabilities	
Current Liabilities	
Accounts Payable	2,317.29
Credit Cards	964.12
Payroll Liabilities	530.34
Line of Credit	4,569.28
Total Current Liabilities	8,381.03
Total Liabilities	8,381.03
Equity	
Owner Contributions	45,800.00
Owner Draws	-44,877.33
Total Owner Capital	922.67
Retained Earnings	9,054.28
Net Income	27,378.09
Total Equity	37,355.04
TOTAL LIABILITIES & EQUITY	45,736.07

Figure 10: Balance Sheet for Doug's Premier Plumbing

Doug's Premier Plumbing, Inc.
Profit & Loss
As of October 31, 2018

	Jan 1 - Oct 31, 2018
Ordinary Income/Expense	
Residential Services	49,238.75
Commercial Services	35,249.22
Total Income	84,487.97
Cost of Goods Sold	
Parts and Materials	16,238.56
Subcontractor Costs	10,175.00
Total COGS	26,413.56
Gross Profit	58,074.41
Expense	
Advertising Expense	450.00
Business License & Fees	75.00
Car/Truck Expense	1,223.17
Charitable Contributions	150.00
Depreciation Expense	846.12
Dues and Subscriptions	175.00
Insurance	4,150.00
Maintenance/Janitorial	1,641.25
Meals, Local	178.25
Office Expenses	1,075.00
Postage and Delivery	0.00
Professional Fees	119.53
Legal Fees	600.00
Accounting Fees	2,319.00
Total Professional Fees	3,038.53
Rent	7,005.00
Repairs and Maintenance	390.00
Telephone	895.24
Payroll Expenses	
Wages	6,576.00
Payroll Tax Expense	2,326.17
Total Payroll Expenses	8,902.17
Utilities	501.59
Total Expense	30,696.32
Net Ordinary Income	27,378.09
Net Income	**27,378.09**

Figure 11: Profit & Loss Statement for Doug's Premier Plumbing

There are many reports that different businesses use, but these two are front and center for *every* business. (A lot of small business owners don't even know their Balance Sheet exists—you are smarter than that!) Your business financial health cannot be determined from a single report alone. You need both the Profit & Loss AND the Balance Sheet together to give you complete feedback. Period.

Let's go into a bit more detail on both of them, starting with my favorite: the Balance Sheet.

The Balance Sheet

When I meet with a new client, I always review the Balance Sheet first. Why? Well, regardless of the size of the business, all of the accounts on the Balance Sheet matter. When those accounts have goofy balances (negative, backward, too high, too low) or don't even exist, I know that the Profit & Loss is wonky too. And, yes, "goofy" and "wonky" are acceptable bookkeeping terms.

If you run a Balance Sheet for your business, you'll see various subtotals: Current Assets, Total Assets, Current Liabilities, Total Liabilities, and Total Equity. Depending on your business and your own situation, you might have more accounts and other subtotals listed.

What I want you to see is that when you file individual transactions in the correct folders, with the right dates, you end up with a report that gives you real information.

Okay, I get it. You feel like you're looking at something written in a foreign language. So now let's teach you enough of that language to get by. It's always good to be able to order another beer or ask for a bathroom/loo/water closet in the native language, right? (And probably in that order.)

Back in Chapter 2 we talked briefly about the Chart of Accounts and we noted that each account in the list falls into a category. That categorization shows up the most when looking at the Balance Sheet. Each of those categories tells part of your business's story. We will walk through a more detailed description of each category and what you'll find there.

Look at the Balance Sheet example again and we can review it in sections.

Assets

At the top, the first section you'll see is Assets. Remember, Assets are what the business owns. You own a bank account, you own the money owed to you in Accounts Receivable, and you might own furniture, fixtures, equipment, and inventory.

Doug's Premier Plumbing, Inc.
Balance Sheet
As of October 31, 2018

	Oct 31, 2018
ASSETS	
Current Assets	
Checking/Savings	
Business Checking	35,457.19
Business Savings	500.00
Total Checking/Savings	35,957.19
Accounts Receivable	
Accounts Receivable	8,125.00
Total Accounts Receivable	8,125.00
Total Current Assets	44,082.19
Fixed Assets	
Computer & Office Equipment	2,500.00
Accumulated Depreciation	-846.12
Total Fixed Assets	1,653.88
TOTAL ASSETS	45,736.07
LIABILITIES & EQUITY	

Figure 12: Balance Sheet – Assets Section

Current Assets is a subcategory of Assets that represents the kind of assets that you could convert to cash within a year. The balances in Current Assets accounts usually revolve, rotate, or change. You buy and sell inventory, so that balance shifts with each purchase or sale. Your Accounts Receivable balance will change as you receive payments from customers, make new sales, or even write off balances as uncollectible.

Bank accounts show up at the top of the Balance Sheet since they are typically every business's primary asset. If the bank account is not reconciled, the balance showing in that account is likely wrong. The process of reconciling the bank accounts (more on that later) ensures that what is in your bookkeeping system matches what the bank says happened.

Here's an example of what happens when you don't reconcile: Say you write your rent check, $1,000, late in the month, a few days before it's due for the next month. And you set it aside until your landlord pops in to pick it up. When they do show up, you can't find the check, so you write out another one. And you do not void the first one . . .

That means that your Rent Expense account is too high (Profit & Loss) and your Cash account (Balance Sheet) is too low—because it looks like you paid rent twice. That is a simplistic example, but it's a real one—I've seen it happen. You get busy and sucked into something else, and you never get back to voiding the check. That unvoided check throws balances off—and those balances are what show up when you run reports. By making sure to reconcile your bank accounts, you can find the unvoided check and any other anomalies.

How about another example using Accounts Receivable? You are a contractor and you invoice a customer for a new deck that is 50% complete. They owe you $5,500 for the first half of the work (Nice deck, I'd like to see pictures!), and when you receive the payment, you deposit it. When you deposit the payment, your bookkeeper records it as income. It increases your bank balance and it increases Income. Right?

Nope, there's a big old "oops" in there. Your bookkeeper should have recorded it as a payment received on the customer's account. That would reduce the balance in Accounts Receivable and increase the balance in Cash. There should be no effect on Income because the invoice to the customer already recorded the income.

If that was confusing, don't freak out. The point is that misrecorded transactions can affect both financial statements, but the Balance Sheet accounts need to be accurate before the Profit & Loss accounts can give you real numbers.

Another category of assets is called Fixed Assets, which are the items you've purchased for your business that have, in accounting lingo, a long "useful life."

You can see on Doug's Balance Sheet that he has computers and equipment listed. If his plumbing business owned a building and land, those would show up in this section too. And when he buys a new truck, it will be recorded in this section.

Fixed assets are those purchased over a threshold amount of either $2,500 or $5,000. Purchases made over the threshold amount are considered depreciable assets; purchases made under the threshold amount are considered expenses. The IRS allows you to choose which threshold to use, so if your business relies on multiple kinds of equipment, vehicles, and tools that cost over $2,500, you'll want to use the $2,500 amount. And if your business is big and has costly assets, you can use the higher cap of $5,000. Remember our guideline about consistency? The threshold you choose isn't something you can bounce back and forth on, so check with your tax professional to make the right choice from the start.

In our example, you will also see an account called Accumulated Depreciation with a negative balance listed. That's okay—that's normal for this account. Depreciation is something that your tax professional will calculate every year on all your equipment, buildings, and vehicles. These types of items are sometimes referred to as Tangible Assets. Depreciation is a means of acknowledging the loss of value due to aging and use.

You can't reduce the original value of the asset because that would rewrite history, i.e., it would change what you paid for the asset. But you can offset the value with an ever-increasing amount of depreciation. The reason I say that your tax professional should calculate depreciation for you is so they can determine the optimal impact on your tax return. Depreciation rules in the U.S. are set by the IRS, and since tax laws change regularly, you need someone who knows the rules to apply them correctly and to your best advantage.

Liabilities

Moving down the Balance Sheet, our next category is Liabilities.

Total Fixed Assets	1,653.88
TOTAL ASSETS	45,736.07
LIABILITIES & EQUITY	
Liabilities	
Current Liabilities	
Accounts Payable	2,317.29
Credit Cards	964.12
Payroll Liabilities	530.34
Line of Credit	4,569.28
Total Current Liabilities	8,381.03
Total Liabilities	8,381.03

Figure 13: Balance Sheet – Liabilities Section

Liabilities are what your business owes, so you see Accounts Payable, Credit Cards, and Payroll Liabilities listed here. This example is simple, but in a more complex business, there might be two sections of Liabilities—Current Liabilities and Long-Term Liabilities.

Current Liabilities is a subcategory of Liabilities that represents amounts owed that will be cleared within a year. Accounts Payable will fall in here; it is a revolving balance of what you owe to people who have sold you products, materials, or services, but there are no long-term financing agreements attached to those debts. Other current liabilities could include a short-term line of credit, Sales Tax Payable, Payroll Liabilities, and possibly Gift Certificates Payable.

In Long-Term Liabilities, you might see a vehicle loan, equipment loans, or other financed loans for which repayment is longer than one year in duration.

Equity

Now let's look at the Equity section.

Equity	
Owner Contributions	45,800.00
Owner Draws	-44,877.33
Total Owner Capital	922.67
Retained Earnings	9,054.28
Net Income	27,378.09
Total Equity	37,355.04
TOTAL LIABILITIES & EQUITY	45,736.07

Figure 14: Balance Sheet – Equity Section

Equity accounts will vary depending on your business structure, but all of these accounts represent the investment you made to start the business, as well as ongoing investments. Equity includes Owner Contributions, Owner Draws (possibly called Owner Withdrawals, Shareholder Distributions, or something similar), Retained Earnings (a cumulative total of profit or loss), and a few other optional accounts depending on how you have funded and withdrawn money from your business.

The equity section is where the business ownership numbers are found, and the terminology is based on the business structure. In Chapter 2 under the Business Structure section, we talked about the terminology of ownership. The effect of entries to ownership may affect your taxes, but that's for your CPA or tax professional to address. I want you to know that when you contribute money to your business or withdraw money from your business, it will show up in this section of the Balance Sheet.

Retained Earnings is a life-to-date rolling total of cumulative profit or loss in the business. If you are a sole proprietorship, you might have an account called Owner's Equity; if you are an LLC it might say Members' Equity. No matter what it's called, it's a balance that is calculated internally by your software. This is the one account I mentioned earlier that does NOT have a register or ledger you can make changes to. You cannot look up the history and activity between date ranges for this account.

SPECIAL NOTE: *Don't ever post directly to Retained Earnings.* "Retained Earnings" might sound like money you can access, but it is not a savings account. You should never have an entry made to this account without direction from your CPA or tax professional. Making an entry essentially rewrites your history, which means you have bogus information on your Balance Sheet, and if you get audited, your taxable income may not match what you reported on a tax return. As you might imagine, auditors do not like to see that . . .

The Value of the Balance Sheet

Now let's look at the Balance Sheet again as a whole. This is where the whole bookkeeping thing comes together successfully (or not). Look at the double lines under Total Assets and again under Total Liabilities & Equity. Notice something about those two numbers?

Yup, you found the accounting equation:

Assets = Liabilities + Equity

The accounting equation . . . Yeah, I know, more math-y stuff. But it's okay—your bookkeeping software is going to sort and balance it all out for you!

One more comment on the Balance Sheet: every account on it rolls forward to the next year. It is the foundational report for your business. While the Profit & Loss statement reflects a date-specific period of activity, the Balance Sheet does not ever reset or start over. It carries forward as long as your business does. Look at the accounts listed on it and you will see why.

The value of the Balance Sheet now should be a little clearer to you. It tells the story of what your business owns and owes, the ownership contributions or withdrawals, and the cumulative earnings (net income or net loss) for the business. That's flippin' EVERYTHING. This is why you start reviewing a business's health on the Balance Sheet, not on the Profit & Loss statement.

If you want a bank loan to pay for some new equipment in your restaurant kitchen, and you only take the bank a copy of your P&L, you are only telling them how much the business earned and spent in a particular time period. If your restaurant turned out an awesome profit of over $50,000 last year, that might look great.

BUT, what if on your Balance Sheet, your accounts are inaccurate? When we acknowledge that the Balance Sheet contains the entire financial story of your business and those accounts have wonky, inaccurate, and backwards numbers, then your Profit & Loss statement cannot have good numbers either.

Let's look at a specific example. You get a power bill and record it to Accounts Payable. That increases your Utilities Expense (Profit & Loss) and it increases your balance in Accounts Payable (Balance Sheet).

Later, you realize you forgot to pay the bill on time, so you whip out a check, handwrite it, and mail it. Your bookkeeper comes along and records the check to Utilities Expense and reduces the bank balance by the amount of the check.

Uh-oh, now your Accounts Payable balance is too high, and your Utilities Expense just doubled. This is a small example, but this kind of mistake made many times over will create wonky Balance Sheet numbers and wonky P&L numbers.

How do you avoid this?

First of all, get a good bookkeeper. They should always check the balance and detail in Accounts Payable before blasting another expense into the system.

Second of all, communicate with your bookkeeper. Make a note on the bill or the check. And finally, when you do your month-end review (more coming on that!), look at what you owe in Accounts Payable and make sure it's accurate.

The Balance Sheet can only tell the true story of your business when all those account balances are correct. When all individual transactions are recorded accurately and by the right date, you get real numbers that a bank—and you—can trust. And because those account balances roll forward in time with you, your Balance Sheet contains the whole financial history of your business.

Profit & Loss Statement

Now let's talk a little about the Profit & Loss statement. That's the one everyone knows and with which they naturally feel the most comfortable. It simply contains the details behind the Net Income amount that shows up on the Balance Sheet.

Let's pause for a minute to review some terminology.

"Income," "revenue," and "profit" are terms that sometimes get used interchangeably, and the term used may vary depending on your bookkeeping software.

- Total Income (as it's called in the QuickBooks images that follow) may also be called Gross Income, Gross Revenue, or just Revenue.
- Gross Profit is usually called Gross Profit (Gross Income minus COGS).
- Net Income may also be called Net Profit or Loss (Gross Profit minus Expenses).

I know it can be confusing, but you'll get used to it.

Back to Doug's Premier Plumbing! Figure 15 on the next page shows Doug's P&L again for reference.

If you look at Doug's current year Balance Sheet, down in the Equity section there is a total of $27,378.09 showing as Net Income. If you run a Profit & Loss statement for the same date, it should provide the same Net Income total, along with the detail that created it.

Doug's Premier Plumbing, Inc.
Profit & Loss
As of October 31, 2018

	Jan 1 - Oct 31, 2018
Ordinary Income/Expense	
Residential Services	49,238.75
Commercial Services	35,249.22
Total Income	84,487.97
Cost of Goods Sold	
Parts and Materials	16,238.56
Subcontractor Costs	10,175.00
Total COGS	26,413.56
Gross Profit	58,074.41
Expense	
Advertising Expense	450.00
Business License & Fees	75.00
Car/Truck Expense	1,223.17
Charitable Contributions	150.00
Depreciation Expense	846.12
Dues and Subscriptions	175.00
Insurance	4,150.00
Maintenance/Janitorial	1,641.25
Meals, Local	178.25
Office Expenses	1,075.00
Postage and Delivery	0.00
Professional Fees	119.53
Legal Fees	600.00
Accounting Fees	2,319.00
Total Professional Fees	3,038.53
Rent	7,005.00
Repairs and Maintenance	390.00
Telephone	895.24
Payroll Expenses	
Wages	6,576.00
Payroll Tax Expense	2,326.17
Total Payroll Expenses	8,902.17
Utilities	501.59
Total Expense	30,696.32
Net Ordinary Income	27,378.09
Net Income	**27,378.09**

Figure 15: Profit & Loss Statement for Doug's Premier Plumbing

Make sense? This is why dates matter on both transactions and reports. When you use the same dates for both reports, then you have a Profit & Loss report that provides the detail of the net profit showing on the Balance Sheet. Let me repeat that for clarity: The net profit or loss (aka Net Income) showing as a single line item on your Balance Sheet is broken down in detail on the Profit & Loss report.

Both reports together tell the story of your business, but the Profit & Loss report breaks out the detail for both your revenue and expenses for the period on the report. This detail gives you important feedback on how you are operating your business. It tells you what your gross profit is, as well as whether or not your sales are high enough to cover your business expenses. As you might guess, that's key to longevity in business—covering your expenses and making a profit.

Let's walk through the Profit & Loss statement section by section. There are basically three sections: Revenue, Cost of Goods Sold, and Expenses.

Revenue (Income)

Everyone knows what Revenue is: money coming into your business from business activities. Revenue is the term for your gross income—that is, what you made before deducting any costs. As noted earlier, "revenue" is frequently used interchangeably with the term "income," but as you'll see, one of two words needs to precede the word "income" to make your use of it clear: "gross" or "net." Gross Income is before COGS and Expenses. Net Income is after COGS and Expenses. Rather than Gross Income, I prefer to use the term Revenue.

The number of ways you break down your revenue has to do with your business and the information needed to analyze it appropriately. I've seen revenue broken down into quite a few accounts—for example, you might have Wholesale Sales, Retail Sales, Online Sales, and Discounted Sales—but you can also choose to have a single category for sales. It is up to you and what kind of summary you want to see for your business.

Doug's Premier Plumbing breaks its revenue down into two types of revenue that are relevant to what Doug wants to know about his sales: Residential Services and Commercial Services. As noted, QuickBooks refers to your revenue number as Total Income, as you can see in Figure 16.

Doug's Premier Plumbing, Inc.
Profit & Loss
As of October 31, 2018

	Jan 1 - Oct 31, 2018
Ordinary Income/Expense	
Residential Services	49,238.75
Commercial Services	35,249.22
Total Income	84,487.97

Figure 16: P&L – Revenue, or Total Income

Now let's look at how expenses are divided on the Profit & Loss statement.

Cost of Goods Sold

First of all, the Cost of Goods Sold (COGS) accounts are listed right below your sales accounts, and the subtotal below that is Gross Profit.

Recall that back in the Chart of Accounts section, I talked briefly about the Cost of Goods Sold accounts. These are special expense accounts for tracking costs that are directly attached to each sale. If you buy products and mark them up and resell them, then the cost of the products sold should show up below your sales accounts on your Profit & Loss statement. (COGS differs from Inventory in that COGS is related to products that have been sold; Inventory includes products purchased but not yet sold.)

COGS does *not* include expenses that you would still have even if you had no sales—things like rent and loan payments still exist even if you don't sell anything. Think of it this way: if you did not have any sales for the whole month, nothing would show up in the COGS line items. So the numbers you want to see here are always sales specific.

You might have several COGS accounts, or you might just have one. It depends on your business and the kind of detail you want to see on your reports. What you need to remember is that when you set up a new account as a Cost of Goods Sold type, it should be directly related to sales.

	Jan 1 - Oct 31, 2018
Ordinary Income/Expense	
Residential Services	49,238.75
Commercial Services	35,249.22
Total Income	84,487.97
Cost of Goods Sold	
Parts and Materials	16,238.56
Subcontractor Costs	10,175.00
Total COGS	26,413.56
Gross Profit	58,074.41

Figure 17: P&L – Cost of Goods Sold

With Doug's Premier Plumbing, the Cost of Goods Sold includes all the parts and materials he puts into each plumbing job, as well as any subcontracted labor he uses for each job. You might also put Credit Card Fees here (also known as Merchant Services), Job Travel, Packaging Supplies, Products Purchased, and so on. Anything you record to this category of costs will be variable—as sales increase, so does Cost of Goods Sold. And as sales decrease, Cost of Goods Sold will drop.

Now look just below the Total Cost of Goods Sold—there's your Gross Profit.

Gross Profit

Gross Profit is your first critical analysis number! Gross Profit is calculated (by your software, so don't panic) by subtracting your COGS from your Total Income (revenue). This number tells you how much you have left over to cover all your other operating costs.

In Doug's case, he has a gross profit of $58,074.41 for the reporting period. He will need that to cover the rest of his business expenses. So let's look at those expenses in the last section on the P&L statement.

Expense

The Expense section of the P&L statement is where all your non-COGS expenses land. (See Figure 18 next page.) These might be called Operating Expenses, Administrative Expenses, or Overhead Expenses. These expenses are costs of doing business; they happen whether you had any sales or not and include things like Rent Expense, Insurance Expense, Payroll Expense, or anything else that you paid to keep your doors open and to make it possible for your business to make sales.

The P&L statement lists all your income and expense account totals (your "file folders"), so remember back when you set up your Chart of Accounts? This is where your choice of account names and account types matters.

Expense	
Advertising Expense	450.00
Business License & Fees	75.00
Car/Truck Expense	1,223.17
Charitable Contributions	150.00
Depreciation Expense	846.12
Dues and Subscriptions	175.00
Insurance	4,150.00
Maintenance/Janitorial	1,641.25
Meals, Local	178.25
Office Expenses	1,075.00
Postage and Delivery	119.53
Professional Fees	0.00
Legal Fees	600.00
Accounting Fees	2,319.00
Total Professional Fees	2,919.00
Rent	7,005.00
Repairs and Maintenance	390.00
Telephone	895.24
Payroll Expenses	
Wages	6,576.00
Payroll Tax Expense	2,326.17
Total Payroll Expenses	8,902.17
Utilities	501.59
Total Expense	30,696.32
Net Ordinary Income	27,378.09
Net Income	**27,378.09**

Figure 18: P&L – Expenses and Net Income

For example, let's say you have a printing business. You do custom flyers, business brochures, business cards, and so on. You have high-quality printers that go through a lot of expensive ink. If you have an account called Office Supplies and you record your ink purchases there, that account total is probably going to be way too high and not accurately reflect the supplies your purchased for use in your own office. You want to record your expenses to the account that most accurately represents what the expenditure was for. So ink purchased specifically for your customer projects should be recorded to a Cost of Goods

Sold account and not with printer ink purchased for the general office printer and recorded as Office Supplies Expense.

Net Income

The very bottom of your Profit & Loss statement is going to be your Net Income, also called Net Profit or Loss, hence the term "the bottom line." Don't freak out if you have a negative balance. That happens in business. A seasonal business may have some months with a negative balance (Net Loss) and some months with a positive balance (Net Profit). It happens—but you need to know why, and whether it is expected or not! As you can see, Doug made a net profit, after all of his expenses, of $27,378.09.

The Value of the Profit & Loss Statement

Think of your Profit & Loss as the detailed feedback report for how income and expenses are cycling through your business. You know from our review of the Balance Sheet that your net income or net loss shows up as a number in the Equity section. If you run a Profit & Loss statement with an end date that matches the one for the Balance Sheet, you will get the details of that net profit or net loss. There are several ways you can use this data.

Making Corrections. Reviewing your P&L statement gives you an opportunity to catch errors and make corrections. COGS is one of those areas that warrants close review, and often requires corrections before closing the month. When you review Cost of Goods Sold, check to make sure that the only costs reported there are direct sales costs. When you include too much in COGS, it distorts your product and service costs.

Then, as you work your way through the operating expenses, check to see if they are aligned with what you expect to see. Check for balances that are too high, too low, or even need to be split out into more accounts to give you better feedback on what you are actually spending.

Back at Doug's Premium Plumbing, Doug should be putting job-specific costs in his Cost of Goods Sold accounts, including items like job materials, plumbing parts, and job-specific labor that went onto each client invoice.

Say Doug is on the way to a customer job and his van breaks down. That event could just as easily have happened on his way to pick up a lunch order; it is not a direct job cost, so it should not be included in Cost of Goods Sold.

On the other hand, a construction modification requires Doug to extend pipes under the master bathroom sink to accommodate a wall that was shifted. His original bid might not have included all the materials or the additional labor, but because he is invoicing for the costs, he can pull additional inventory and add that as a job cost.

Identifying New Reporting Needs. Over time your accounting needs may change. The P&L can help flag when changes are warranted.

For example, Doug might initially record business supplies to an account called Supplies Expense. As the business grows and costs increase, one account might not provide enough information. Doug might decide to bust out the Supplies Expense account into Office Supplies, Shop Supplies, and Truck Supplies for better information. That new level of detail will tell Doug how much is actually being spent in each area. Then, if Truck Supplies—which includes small tools, limited inventory,

O-rings, bibb washers, and so on—starts creeping up, Doug can follow up to see if his crews are charging enough to cover all those incidental costs. Or if they are losing tools off the back of the truck . . .

Calculating Profitability Ratios. One use of the P&L is to analyze your business by calculating profitability ratios such as Gross Profit Margin and Net Profit Margin. These ratios indicate how much of your sales revenue goes to cover expenses and how much is left as profit. When you have these numbers, you can compare them with the ratios achieved by other businesses in your industry—are you achieving above- or below-average profitability? That can then lead you to business decisions about pricing, expenses, and so on that can improve your profitability. We'll go into details about calculating ratios in Chapter 8.

Are you starting to see why all your numbers matter? All those numbers flow in from minor, everyday transactions, and then come together to give you feedback that you can use in real-life, daily business decisions. It ain't magic. It's business.

The Statement of Cash Flows

The Balance Sheet and P&L give you valuable feedback from which you can decide what business adjustments to make. There's one more financial statement that can be useful but often gets overlooked: the Statement of Cash Flows (SCF).

The Statement of Cash Flows is a report that summarizes where cash and cash equivalents have come in and gone out of the company during a given period. It starts with your Net Income for the period, then reconciles that to the net increase or decrease in cash for the period. Recall that when you work on an accrual system, you don't always get cash when a sale is made, and you don't always send cash out when a purchase is made. This report shows you what happened with the actual cash (and equivalents).

Now I'm going to admit something to you that might be surprising coming from a bookkeeper: I find the Statement of Cash Flows to be a bit confusing. So if you find this report difficult to follow, you're not alone. But hang in there . . .

Take a look at Doug's SCF in Figure 19 (next page).

The SCF sorts activities into three categories: operating activities, investing activities, and financing activities.

If you look near the bottom, you will see he started the period with $12,318.20 in cash.

Now go to the top and you'll see Doug had Net Income of $18,962.20 for the period.

In the Operating Activities section, we see where money has come in or gone out from business operations. Doug subtracts Accounts Receivable because he is still waiting on customers to pay him $8,125 that is owed (if it's in A/R, he doesn't have the cash yet, right?). And he adds his current liabilities (Accounts Payable, Credit Card, Line of Credit, and Payroll Liabilities) because he is still holding that cash (he owes it but hasn't paid it yet, right?).

So the cash provided by operations for that period was $19,218.23. Notice that *cash provided is not the same as his net income.*

Stay with me here . . .

In the Investment Activities section, we look at things that cause money to come in or go out with the purpose of growing your business. For example, buying a vehicle or a piece of equipment is an investment to grow your business; selling the vehicle or equipment is a divestment (opposite of investment).

Doug's Premier Plumbing
Statement of Cash Flows
January through March 2018

	Jan - Mar 18
OPERATING ACTIVITIES	
Net Income	18,962.20
Adjustments to reconcile Net Income to net cash provided by operations:	
Accounts Receivable	-8,125.00
Accounts Payable	2,317.29
Credit Card	964.12
Line of Credit	4,569.28
Payroll Liabilities	530.34
Net cash provided by Operating Activities	19,218.23
INVESTING ACTIVITIES	
Accumulated Depreciation	40,131.29
Automobiles & Trucks	-45,000.00
Computer & Office Equipment	-2,500.00
Net cash provided by Investing Activities	-7,368.71
FINANCING ACTIVITIES	
Truck Loan	14,130.72
Owner Contributions	45,800.00
Owner Draws	-44,877.33
Retained Earnings	9,054.28
Net cash provided by Financing Activities	24,107.67
Net cash increase for period	35,957.19
Cash at beginning of period	12,318.20
Cash at end of period	**48,275.39**

Figure 19: Statement of Cash Flows for Doug's Premier Plumbing

In looking at Doug's example, you can see that he bought a new truck and some new office equipment (cash out). You will also notice Depreciation, which reduces the value of tangible assets, shows up in the investment activity section (sounds goofy, but it's the equivalent of cash in—again, let your accountant worry about the depreciation calculation). As a result, Investing Activities reduced his cash balance by $7,368.71.

In the Financing Activities section, we look at things like making loan payments, putting money into your business, or withdrawing money from your business. You'll also notice Retained Earnings, which we mentioned earlier. (Don't touch!)

In Doug's case, he took out a truck loan that added to his cash balance, and he made owner contributions and owner draws that were close to a wash. All in all, his Financing Activities added $24,107.67 to his cash balance.

So recall Doug started the period with a cash balance of $12,318.20.

Operations added to cash by $19,218.23. Investing reduced cash by $7,368.71. And Financing added to cash by $24,107.67.

At the end of the period, Doug's cash balance has gone up $35,957.19 to a new balance of $48,275.39.

The Statement of Cash Flows does *not* give you the full financial picture for your business, and for many stable businesses, the SCF may not be particularly helpful. I run it most often when I have a client say, "I can't have a net profit—my bank account is too low!" Yes, you can have a profit without cash, and cash without a profit.

The SCF can also be helpful for cash-intensive businesses or businesses that are growing rapidly, and if your P&L is showing a net loss, the SCF can help determine which types of activities are driving the loss.

As I said, this is a tricky report, so if you are having trouble following it, ask your financial professional to interpret it for you.

Chapter Summary

The entire flow of data and numbers in your business gets summarized in two financial statements: the Balance Sheet and the Profit & Loss statement. The Balance Sheet shows assets, liabilities, and equity. The P&L shows revenue, expenses, and profit (or loss).

Your Chart of Accounts is the index to how your data is filed, and the way it is organized will be reflected on both the Balance Sheet and the Profit & Loss. The complexity of the reports is up to you, but ideally you want to arrange your accounts to give you usable feedback in the form of summarized categories.

Learn to review your Balance Sheet first, because if anything is entered wrong or not recorded at all, it will show up on the Balance Sheet first. If the Balance Sheet accounts have bad numbers or invalid balances, then you cannot trust the details on the Profit & Loss statement.

A third financial statement, the Statement of Cash Flows, is useful in analyzing how cash and cash equivalents have moved through your business.

5
Other Reports

Using accounting software gives you access to all kinds of reports that are useful in reviewing your business. Most will also allow you to review them on-screen, and then click down into layers of detail. Because accounting software varies beyond what I can (and want to) discuss here, I'll just give you an overview of some of the reports my clients and I have found useful.

Account History Reports

An Account History, or in QuickBooks a Transaction Detail Report, will list out the activity in an account—it's like pulling out a file folder and seeing what's in it. This is a good way to review an expense account that seems high. If all your transaction data has been filled in completely (who you paid, for what, when, and so on), then you will be able to review and see if something should be coded to a different account.

Example: You review your Profit & Loss and see that your Insurance Expense account is higher than usual. You know you pay about $1,375 twice a year for liability and auto insurance, and your account total appears to be about $2,000 too high. In looking at the Account History for the year, you can see payments for the liability and auto insurance, but, oops, there's also a $2,000 payment to your attorney. That one clearly needs to be reclassed, or recoded, to Professional Fees/Legal Expense. Making that correction will give you a better idea of what you are really paying for Insurance Expense as well as for Legal Expense.

Doug's Premier Plumbing
Transaction Detail By Account
January 1 through October 31, 2018

	Type	Date	Num	Name	Debit	Credit	Balance
Insurance Expense							
	Check	03/21/2018	5341	Standard Insurance Company	1,375.00		4,750.00
	Check	04/30/2018	5422	ABC LawFirm	2,000.00		
	Check	09/25/2018	5891	Standard Insurance Company	1,375.00		
Total Insurance					4,750.00	0.00	4,750.00
TOTAL					4,750.00	0.00	4,750.00

Figure 20: Transaction Detail with a Miscoded Item

This Account History or Transaction Detail report is a basic way to dial in to the details of what makes up the total costs in your various accounts. As you move through your year in a busy business, it's easy to forget where your costs come from and where the money goes. Use this report to refresh your memory as well as to look for corrections that need to be made.

Payroll Summary

A Payroll Summary will give you an overview of what your payroll costs are by employee, by pay period, by month, or by several other options. The summary lists Gross Wages, payroll deductions, Net Pay, and then, depending on your settings, the associated company costs for taxes. I run a payroll summary for each payroll I process, and then I use it to calculate the payroll tax deposit.

Doug's Premier Plumbing
Payroll Summary
January through March 2018

	Hours	Rate	Jan - Mar 18
Employee Wages, Taxes and Adjustments			
Gross Pay			
Owner salary	225.00		7,500.00
Hourly Wages	125.00	22.50	2,812.50
Total Gross Pay	350.00		10,312.50
Adjusted Gross Pay	350.00		10,312.50
Taxes Withheld			
Federal Withholding			-1,237.50
Medicare Employee			-149.53
Social Security Employee			-639.38
Workers Comp			-25.88
Medicare Employee Addl Tax			0.00
Total Taxes Withheld			-2,052.29
Net Pay	350.00		**8,260.21**
Employer Taxes and Contributions			
Federal Unemployment			61.88
Medicare Company			149.53
Social Security Company			639.38
State Unemployment			128.89
Workers Compensation			117.45
Total Employer Taxes and Contributions			**1,097.13**

Figure 21: Payroll Summary Report

This report in QuickBooks can include individual names, and the date range can be customized. For a single payroll, use just the pay date. This will give you a snapshot picture of what your payroll costs are. Figure 22 shows how I summarize a pending payroll tax deposit.

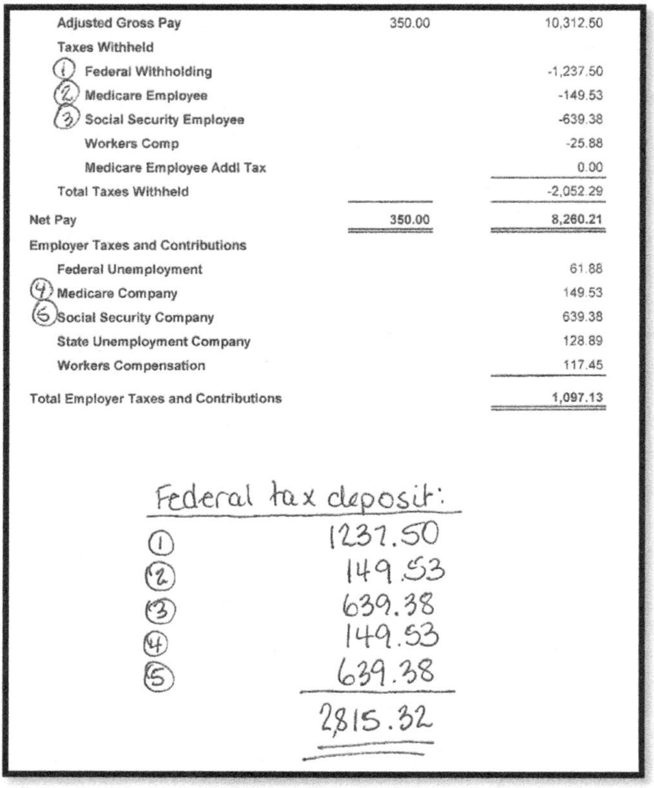

Adjusted Gross Pay	350.00	10,312.50
Taxes Withheld		
(1) Federal Withholding		-1,237.50
(2) Medicare Employee		-149.53
(3) Social Security Employee		-639.38
Workers Comp		-25.88
Medicare Employee Addl Tax		0.00
Total Taxes Withheld		-2,052.29
Net Pay	350.00	8,260.21
Employer Taxes and Contributions		
Federal Unemployment		61.88
(4) Medicare Company		149.53
(5) Social Security Company		639.38
State Unemployment Company		128.89
Workers Compensation		117.45
Total Employer Taxes and Contributions		1,097.13

Federal tax deposit:

(1)	1237.50
(2)	149.53
(3)	639.38
(4)	149.53
(5)	639.38
	2815.32

Figure 22: Payroll Summary with Tax Deposit

You'll notice the handwriting is where I've pulled out the totals for the federal tax deposit and tallied them. This is a good way to track what you will need to set aside for the tax deposit. If you have a good bookkeeper, you can ask for this information to keep on top of what you are paying, when you are paying it, and in some cases, that it's getting paid at all.

Payroll tax is not something to be complacent about. I know of one business in which the owners assumed wrongly that their qualified bookkeeper was making all the right tax deposits.

When the unpaid taxes finally came to light, the business ended up closing. In that case, the owners re-formed, started over, and repaid all the back taxes. Don't let this be you—follow up on your own, and review your data.

Again, use reports, get the information from your bookkeeper, and take the initiative to see that your payroll tax payments are made on time. The responsibility will ultimately land on you as the business owner, so of all the business processes you need to manage, this is one of the most critical.

Sales Tax Liability Report

I use the Sales Tax Liability report each month when I file various tax returns. This report lets you know how much sales tax you have collected. Due to the variation in how tax is collected and remitted in different locales, this report needs to be set up correctly from the beginning, so it might be helpful to find an accounting pro who is local to your place of business and familiar with your accounting software.

When the report is set up correctly, you will be able to see a list of taxable sales and the tax liability reported by region/city. Sales tax is specific to where you are located and how you do business (one location, or delivery to multiple intrastate and interstate locations). Ensure you have qualified help on sales tax, but don't delegate to the point that you have no visibility or access to it. Like payroll, this is something that needs to be paid on time or you will risk accruing penalties and interest.

As I mentioned in a previous section, one way to help yourself keep current is to set up a separate bank account for taxes—specifically, payroll and sales tax. Transfer funds to it as you know what you owe, and then you'll be confident you're covered.

Undeposited Funds Report

The Undeposited Funds report tells you how much is pending in credit card payments that have yet to be settled. It also tells you how much you have received through your point-of-sale (POS) system that needs to be deposited. Most business insurance policies have some kind of limit on the amount of insured cash on hand. If you are not the one responsible for making daily or weekly bank deposits, you'll want to know how much cash is sitting around waiting to be deposited. And this might be a good way to know when your business has grown enough to need a policy change.

Banking and Bank Reconciliation Reports

Various banking reports can be helpful as well. These may be as simple as a screen print for a fast review, or you can save and print your bank reconciliation reports to attach to your bank statements. For some clients, I never print bank reports, but for others, I print and save all of them. The value of bank reports depends on you and your business—a complex business with high-volume sales might need more review and monitoring than a small business with less frequent sales.

A bank register report doesn't even need to be printed to be helpful. Review it daily to see how your books compare to the bank balance if you have a high volume of daily sales, or review it monthly or quarterly if your sales transactions are less frequent. I do quick reviews for several clients using this approach, as it's an easy way to catch errors and fix them.

I'll talk about reconciliations a bit later, but I want to mention here that they are useful reports to review. Bank reconciliations tie what happened in your accounting records to what happened at the bank on your account. The reconciliation report should be reviewed because it will tell you if there are any deposits or payments that have not yet cleared the bank. If you are not the one doing your own bank reconciliations, I would recommend reviewing them. If you have checks from two years ago that haven't cleared your bank account yet, they probably need to be voided and reissued. A missing deposit that's taking too long to show up probably means it hasn't made it to the bank, has been recorded to the wrong bank account, or any number of things.

Use a bank reconciliation report to find errors and get them fixed.

Sales by Customer

Sales by Customer is a handy report because it will tell you, based on your date ranges, what your sales totals are by customer. This could give you some surprising feedback if you aren't sure which customers are accounting for the highest sales.

If you use a cash register or point-of-sale system and do not track sales by customer name, then you might benefit from running Sales by Day or some other time frame. Tracking sales trends will tell you when your sales are the highest and lowest, and which days create the most demand on your time and your staff's time. This is a good planning tool.

Aging Reports

Nope, Aging Reports aren't about aching joints and foggy memories. "Aging" is a bookkeeping term used for both Accounts Receivable (A/R) and Accounts Payable (A/P) to see when something was due and if it is past due.

An Accounts Receivable Aging report spreads out customer invoices by the due date, typically in 30-day increments. This lets you clearly see who is not paying you on time. It is a good way to get a look at what you are owed and when the funds should be coming in based on the due date.

Doug's Premier Plumbing
A/R Aging Summary
As of October 31, 2018

	Current	1 - 30	31 - 60	61 - 90	> 90	TOTAL
Ace Landscaping	3,120.00	0.00	0.00	0.00	0.00	3,120.00
Jones Family	1,250.00	1,250.00	0.00	0.00	0.00	2,500.00
Smith Family	2,505.00	0.00	0.00	0.00	0.00	2,505.00
TOTAL	**6,875.00**	**1,250.00**	**0.00**	**0.00**	**0.00**	**8,125.00**

Figure 23: Accounts Receivable Aging Summary

Watching this report can help you reduce time delays on getting payments from slow customers. The frequency with which you run it will depend on your business and how often you make sales. You might want to run it every Monday and then tell your staff to hold off on making any sales to any customers who are falling behind.

The Accounts Payable Aging report is similar, but it shows what YOU owe and when you owe it. It can help you plan and schedule payments to vendors and suppliers when cash flow is tight.

Doug's Premier Plumbing
A/P Aging Summary
As of October 31, 2018

	Current	1 - 30	31 - 60	61 - 90	> 90	TOTAL
A. Disposal Service	51.29	0.00	0.00	0.00	0.00	51.29
Something Power Company	0.00	256.78	0.00	0.00	0.00	256.78
Basic Plumbing Supplies	561.85	1,447.37	0.00	0.00	0.00	2,009.22
TOTAL	613.14	1,704.15	0.00	0.00	0.00	2,317.29

Figure 24: Accounts Payable Aging Summary

One more thing I want to say about both the Accounts Receivable Summary and the Accounts Payable Summary reports: watch your dates for reporting periods. Both of these report totals should always match the totals on the Balance Sheet. If there are errors or problems in your bookkeeping, make sure your dates match; if you still don't see an absolute match, you might need some professional help.

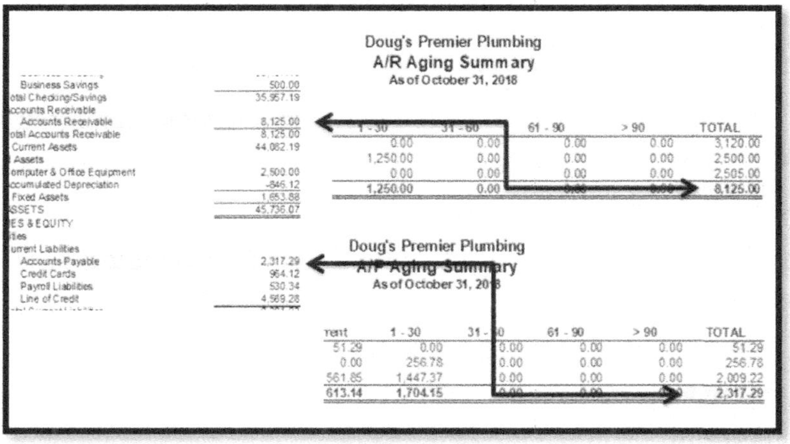

Figure 25: A/R and A/P Details Match the Balance Sheet

Chapter Summary

Reports are the basic feedback mechanism for your business. They will capture and summarize all those transactions you've successfully recorded by date and account. While the Balance Sheet and the Profit & Loss statement are key, there are many other reports that your accounting software can provide.

Helpful customer reports include the Sales by Customer if your sales are individually invoiced. Or you can use the A/R Aging report to show you who owes you what—you can use it to plan your cash flow or to put slow-paying customers on hold.

Payroll Summary reports and the Sales Tax Liability both work to help you plan cash flow and tax payments. The A/P Aging report is also a good cash flow planning tool as it tells you what you owe and when you owe it. Make sure your bookkeeper is entering accurate due dates on the bills.

Other reports you may find useful include banking reports such as the Undeposited Funds report and the Bank Reconciliation report. Both of those will tell you what has yet to be recorded as received funds, and if there are old checks or deposits that haven't cleared.

With a good software system and good numbers, you can pull reports that explain totals or give you answers to specific questions.

6

Managing Cash Flow

Cash flow is the business reality that determines whether you will stay in business or not. Cash flow is simply a question of timing: When your bills are due, do you have enough cash on hand to pay them? It is that simple.

Your business can survive and even grow while recording a net loss, but if you do not have positive cash flow, it will not survive. If you feel like your business is struggling, focus on cash flow rather than on profit.

That probably doesn't sound like what you've heard or learned, but cash flow is king. I'm going to repeat myself here: cash flow means you know when and how the money is due to come in, and you also know how and when it will go out. If you put your attention on cash flow, you will always know what is due, when it is due, and when you will receive money to pay it. That's an amazingly strong foundation for any business!

Cash flow is a challenge for a lot of business owners (and let me be clear, it's an ongoing challenge, not a one-and-done kind of thing), but once you master it, the rest of your business is primed for growth and you can turn your attention to profit.

Understanding cash flow is simple. The matter of managing and tracking cash flow is a bit more complicated. Managing your cash flow means you are aware of what you will receive either in daily sales or in Accounts Receivable as customer invoices become due. Here are several ways you can help yourself manage your cash flow.

Create Separate Bank Accounts

Create separate bank accounts for certain key expenses like payroll and payroll taxes, property taxes, large annual expenses like insurance, and monthly or quarterly sales tax filings. I know—it sounds like you're making things more complicated, but hear me out.

Let's say you own the building in which your business operates. Your annual property taxes are likely paid twice a year and might account for a fairly heavy hit to your bank account. If you set up a bank account to hold the funds until they are due, you can transfer the monthly equivalent into the account until you are ready to pay the bill. A monthly amount is likely to be easier to handle than a semi-annual jolt to your cash. And depending on how revenue flows into your business, maybe even weekly transfers are best for you. (Seem familiar? This is similar to the escrow account on your mortgage. Your monthly payment usually includes principal, interest, insurance, and property taxes; the loan company holds the funds for insurance and property taxes until they are due.) Those big annual or semi-annual costs are tough on cash flow. Setting aside funds in smaller chunks gives you more control. It also leaves you more breathing room in your operating cash.

Payroll can be especially challenging. The process of payroll includes deducting taxes from your employees' gross pay. Spending it instead of remitting it to the appropriate tax agency is unethical, not to mention illegal. And if you fall behind on payroll taxes, your business is in trouble. When you use a separate bank account for payroll and payroll tax funds, you can issue paychecks to employees from it as well as hold funds in it for the taxes when they come due. If you add only one extra bank account to your business, this would be the one I'd encourage you to consider.

Yes, creating separate bank accounts does add some additional detail and complication to your business, but it can also offer you the assurance that you have funds set aside for what you will owe.

Create a Budget

"Creating a budget sounds like fun," said no one ever. But even a simple budget will help you predict what your business revenue will be and what you will owe. QuickBooks Desktop has a budget function that is easy to use, and once you've entered budget numbers, you can run a report that will compare those numbers to your actual numbers. If you use QuickBooks Online, the availability of budget functions depends on your subscription level. Chances are, your accounting software has a built-in budget function, but if not, there also are plenty of online spreadsheets available; just do a quick online search for budget templates.

I get that budgets are "nerd fun" and likely not fun for you if you're reading this book. But maybe you don't need a budget that goes line by line through every single account. Maybe you can get by with a simple budget for monthly revenue, monthly Cost of Goods Sold, and monthly operating expenses.

There. Now you're down to three lines for 12 months—that's only 36 numbers. You can do that! I'm confident you can.

Review History

Something else that will help you manage your cash flow is to review your financial history. In particular, look at your P&L and Statement of Cash Flows to see what revenues, expenses, and other activities (like investment or financing) have affected your cash flow.

Compare year to year to see what has come in and what has gone out. Our lives move quickly, and it is easy to forget where we've been and how far we've come. Run financial statements for prior business years and see where your costs and revenues have increased or decreased.

Reviewing your financial history will also make it easier to estimate what your cash needs will be and what will be available to work with. Use your history to help you.

Monitor Your A/R and A/P

Just because the revenue is booked on a sale (which will increase your profit), it does not mean you will receive it on a timely basis (there's the hit to your cash flow), so monitor your Accounts Receivable for slow-paying customers. Knowing what you are owed and who owes you will enable you to encourage customers to pay on time. Maybe you need to tighten up your payment policies or even turn some non-paying customers over for collection.

Also pay attention to your Accounts Payable. If your bookkeeper records bills as they come into the business and uses the due dates, then you can tell exactly what you owe and when you owe it. Most accounting software programs will let you choose settings that will age it out by the due date: bills due in 0–30 days, 31–60 days, 60–90 days, and so on. From there you can see how much cash you will need to have on hand to cover what you owe.

Ensure Adequate Startup and Operating Capital

One other thing I'm going to address here is the issue of startup capital and operating capital. Both are subjects for a different book, but lack of both can cripple your cash flow.

Startup capital is the funding you had available to start your business. It was what you used to lease your space, buy starting inventory, cover the cost of permits or licenses, buy manufacturing equipment, purchase packaging materials, pay for signage, and so on.

The source of funds you had to set up and start your business can affect daily operating cash flow once your business is up and running. If you financed most of your startup costs, then you must make loan payments out of what your business is earning. And making a large loan payment every month can take a big part of your sales revenue. Part of working with your cash flow is covering both your current operating expenses and the payments you must make over time for previous purchases made via credit (loans and credit cards).

Operating capital is the money you need to operate your business. Early in the life of your business, as you built up your client base, you probably weren't generating enough revenue to fully cover that amount. So in addition to having startup capital, you usually need to have set some funds aside to cover operating expenses until your revenue is high enough to do so. Think of operating capital as the financial buffer that gives your business time to generate enough sales to cover all your costs.

I have no data at hand for this, but I suspect that a lot of small business failures are due to lack of adequate startup capital or operating capital. If you started your business with too little capital, then you may be struggling to make it up now in normal operations. No judgment here for how you started! It happens. But just be aware that it adds to the challenge of cash flow management. You may be making a loan payment or considering taking on additional debt to "catch up." I strongly suggest you work with a business strategist or consultant to find the most cost-effective ways to work through your cash flow challenges.

Chapter Summary

Cash flow is king. A business can survive with a net operating loss for longer than it can survive without cash flow.

Cash flow management requires attention and care from you, but you can help yourself by creating separate bank accounts for specific, isolated purposes, using a budget, reviewing your financial history, monitoring Accounts Receivable, and scheduling Accounts Payable.

Starting your business with low startup or operating capital can create cash flow challenges that last well into business operations. Consider working with a qualified professional to dig out of business debt.

7

A Month in the Life

Invoices to clients, bank statements, incoming bills to pay, loan payments, and each of those transactions we've already discussed all come with a date attached. That date (the drawer in your bookkeeping file cabinet) is where you file your transactions. Those compiled transactions are then sorted into reports that give you valuable feedback on your business.

As a rock-solid business owner, you track a monthly cycle of activity and then review it to see how your business performed. At the end of each month, there is a routine that any decent bookkeeper will work through on your behalf, and you should understand it, even if you don't do it yourself.

Month-End Checklist

One of my favorite tools for working on a client's books is a monthly checklist. It gives me a system of checks and balances (that's a little pun-ish—sorry!) to make sure I don't forget anything. And because each client's business varies, I customize the list.

If you have a bookkeeper on your payroll, or even if you have a contract bookkeeper like me come in a couple of times a month, you can use a monthly checklist as a process-management tool. Your bookkeeper might be responsible for the first few items on the list, or for most of the items. But once it's handed off to you as the business owner, you can use it to make sure various functions inside your business are being accomplished as you expect.

So what might you want on a monthly checklist?

I'd start by making sure all sales activity has been recorded. Then I'd make sure that all bills have been received and booked into Accounts Payable. Those two steps immediately give you the confidence that your revenue and what you owe are both current.

Maybe you want on-hand inventory valued and verified. Or you want a raw materials inventory completed.

Then bank accounts and credit cards need to be reconciled. I'll clarify the need for reconciliations in the next section, but any time there is a third-party statement (banks, credit cards, loans, etc.) on an account, it should be reconciled.

Once all the tasks have been checked off, you should receive the checklist with all the reports you've requested for the month attached. Your checklist can be the cover sheet that assures you that your staff has done what you've requested of them, and your month-end financial statements and reports prove it to you.

In Figure 26 (next page) you'll see a sample checklist.

Doug's Premier Plumbing
Monthly Checklist

Month Ended: ______________________

- [ ] Enter all bills
- [ ] Enter all sales and customer invoices
- [ ] Reconcile bank accounts
- [ ] Reconcile credit cards
- [ ] Reconcile loans payable
- [ ] Print and review Balance Sheet
- [ ] Print and review Profit & Loss Statement
- [ ] Verify Accounts Payable balance
- [ ] Verify Accounts Receivable balance
- [ ] Verify Payroll Liabilities account balance
- [ ] Verify Sales Tax and other tax liability balances
- [ ] Make any adjustments or corrections
- [ ] File and pay any monthly taxes
- [ ] ______________________
- [ ] ______________________
- [ ] ______________________
- [ ] Review and print adjusted/corrected financial statements
- [ ] Enter close date on month

Quarterly:

- [ ] Print and file 941 and make payment
- [ ] File and pay state payroll taxes
- [ ] Make FUTA deposit

Annually:

- [ ] Print, file and pay 940 (FUTA)
- [ ] Print/file employee W-2s and 1099s
- [ ] Print/file federal copies of W-2s and 1099s
- [ ] File and pay any state tax returns
- [ ] Update payroll tax rates in your payroll system for next year

Figure 26: Sample Monthly Checklist

Perform Reconciliations

Okay, reconciliations. I know you've heard that word, but it simply means this: making sure your accounting records match monthly statements from external sources. That can include loan statements, bank statements, credit card statements, and so on.

Bank Reconciliation. Accounting software programs have a specific function that completes the reconciliation process. If you use QuickBooks Online, Xero, or another cloud-based system, the reconciliation process is almost completed as an ongoing function from a bank feed. Desktop software will be a little bit behind the bank without a live feed, but the process is essentially the same. Deposits and payments are checked off against the bank statements, and when you complete the function in your software (press the Reconcile button), it will "clear" the items and mark them as done.

In the old days, bank transactions were frequently keyed in by hand, and errors happened. One reason for reconciling was to make sure that you caught bank errors as soon as possible. Now you are much less likely to see a bank error, though they do happen. (I had a client tell me her employee's bank cashed his paycheck for $20 more than it had been written for. Neither the employee's bank nor my client's bank wanted to bother with correcting it! I helped her adjust her books showing the employee got $20 more than his paycheck had been issued for. Yup, it happens.)

Whether you decide to reconcile your accounts yourself or you expect your bookkeeper to, it's a step that should have owner review. Reviewing the reconciliation will give you a chance to make sure that there are no old payments waiting to be settled out of your bank account, and you can review to see if your various bank and credit card balances match your books.

Loan Reconciliation. Something else that is important in reconciling is ensuring that loan payments are being recorded properly. If you have a loan with a financial institution, you likely borrowed according to agreed terms: interest rate, length of the loan, and the amount of the payment.

When you make a loan payment, the transaction record needs to be split appropriately between interest and principal. If the entire payment is recorded against the loan principal, the balance on your books drops far too quickly and will not match what the bank says you owe.

Getting a copy of a loan schedule or amortization schedule will give you the proper split for principal and interest for the life of the loan. If your bookkeeper has never asked you for it or has never reconciled your loan, then I'm going to say very directly that you need a new bookkeeper. This is a hot-button issue with me, and it is one of the most frequent errors I need to fix when I follow a bad bookkeeper.

Any loan made to your business needs to be reconciled. That will ensure you are getting the right amount of interest expense recorded every month, but also that the actual amount you still owe on the loan matches what the financial institution says you owe.

And I'll go one step further with this: if you have a personal loan from family or a private entity, get a loan schedule and reconcile that as well. This is a professional way to keep things clear and remain accountable.

Print and Review Financial Statements

After all your transactional and other business activity is done for the month and you've made sure everything is caught up, the next thing on your Awesome Business Owner To-Do List is to print out the financial statements and review them.

Print, or have your bookkeeper print, the following:

- Balance Sheet
- Profit & Loss
- Statement of Cash Flows
- Accounts Receivable Summary
- Accounts Payable Summary

Make sure all the reports have the same month-end date. With the Profit & Loss statement, you can ask for a year-to-date and a month-only report. That way you can look at the big picture as well as the previous month as a standalone period.

Okay, now that you've got the reports, what do you review? I know everyone wants to go straight to the bottom line on the Profit & Loss. My recommendation is to go to the Balance Sheet first.

Start at the top and look at each account and its balance. Ask yourself: Does this look correct? Even if you don't know, you're on the right track. Once you do this for several months in a row, it will get easier and errors will stand out more quickly.

While you're looking at the Balance Sheet, you can compare your Accounts Receivable Summary and Accounts Payable Summary to the totals. They should match (we covered that earlier). Both summary reports should give you the detail that supports the totals on the Balance Sheet. That way you know who owes you and who you owe, and you can immediately verify that you've got good numbers.

Go through the rest of the Balance Sheet accounts and ask your bookkeeper for any explanations you feel you need. I'm going to say again that a good bookkeeper will explain the totals. Loans should be reconciled to loan statements regularly. Bank accounts should have been reconciled and old transactions corrected or updated. Depreciation might only change once a year when your tax professional gives your bookkeeper the amounts, but otherwise, you should start to get familiar with what's recorded and how it shows up on your Balance Sheet.

The next report to review is the Profit & Loss statement, and you know what to look for there. Check your revenue, check your Cost of Goods Sold. Review each expense account. Maybe your inventory (Balance Sheet account) needs to be adjusted, and that will affect Cost of Goods Sold. If you have items that are no longer in inventory, then the value of those should show up as Cost of Goods Sold, unless you donated or removed inventory for a purpose other than sales.

Finally, does the bottom line look like what you expected? If not, then maybe consider the following:

- Are your sales being recorded accurately and in the right time frames?
- Do you need to break expense accounts out into more detail for better information?
- Is your profit margin too low?
- Can your bookkeeper give you any other information, assistance, or guidance in creating more profit?

The process of reviewing your financial statements can be quick, or it can be done in more depth. What works for you will be based on the size and complexity of your business. I can just promise you that doing this every month will make it easier and quicker over time.

Close the Month

The next part of the monthly cycle of business accounting and bookkeeping is to close the month. This doesn't mean not being able to make corrections past this point, but now it's time to be more aware of dates and timing.

If you report income to any tax agencies on a monthly, quarterly, or annual basis, they likely retain the right to audit your books. Once you've reported income or payroll data, you do not want to go back and make a correction that changes that data. If you do, you'll need to file an amended report.

So the way you keep yourself from accidentally changing reported and taxed data is to close the accounting month. I can't tell you how every software program handles this, but QuickBooks Desktop and QuickBooks Online both use a close date. Xero uses a lock date. The close date or lock date is the end of the month, and it will prevent data changes. This is a function that I strongly recommend using. Date errors happen, and those lock/close dates can be removed or overridden, but at least you have to think about it before you do.

In QuickBooks, to find the close date function, from the Company menu, choose Set Closing Date . . . You should see a button called Set Date/Password (or similar). You can enter a close date with or without a password. I usually do use a password and use the client's street address number or post office box number—just four or five digits like a bank PIN. What this will do is give you a pop-up notice if you accidentally key in a date that is in a closed accounting period. If your intended date is correct and you DO need to change a closed period, you can simply move past the close date function by entering the password.

Chapter Summary

A month is the smallest chunk of the business financial cycle, and using a checklist is a good way to be systematic and consistent in how you review and approve a month's data.

Reconciling third-party statements to bank accounts, loan accounts, and credit card accounts is necessary to make sure your books match what your financial institutions' records show.

Printing and reviewing financial statements allows you to look for errors, inconsistencies, and successes.

Closing the month usually means entering into your bookkeeping system a close date and a simple password or PIN. This prevents data changes and date goofs. Close dates can be overridden if necessary, but it should happen only rarely.

8
Evaluating the Health of Your Business

When you monitor your business on any given day, you are probably working *inside* it in some capacity. You might deal with customers, handle employee or hiring issues, make product decisions, and worry about sales dropping off. Occasionally you need to step back from your daily duties, go *outside* your business, and give yourself time to review the bigger data picture.

The business term for checkpoints inside your business from which you collect feedback is "key performance indicators," or KPIs. Key performance indicators are measurable, meaningful metrics for your business. When you review KPIs for your own business, you will get feedback on what makes sense or matters to you. You can track them and monitor them, which will help you see trends and cycles that you might otherwise overlook.

Using KPIs is like doing an EKG (electrocardiogram, used to test heart function) for your business. When you monitor your physical health by measuring blood pressure, blood sugar, weight, and various other things doctors insist on checking, you have the chance to learn to live better. Checking your business's KPIs gives you the chance to play doctor for your business. Your business health is up to you. Yes, outside factors can throw challenges and even tragedy our way, but businesses are adaptable and changeable—and the sooner you become aware of a business health issue, the sooner you can adjust.

The discussion of all the business KPIs you could monitor would fill a book on its own, so because we're talking about bookkeeping and accounting, I'm going to stick with basic financial metrics and KPIs for examples. But be aware that there are metrics for sales, HR, employment/payroll, inventory, accounts payable, e-commerce, help desk, customer service, social media, and on and on and on.

I'll go through a few KPIs I use with clients, and I'll give you a few more you can consider using on your own. When you start tracking KPIs for your own business, I suggest using a spreadsheet and capturing your results for each week, month, or quarter.

And one other thing: to preserve your sanity, keep it simple to start. I know it can be tempting to go all in when you start something new, but I would rather see you succeed on something small to start with than do a virtual face-plant by tackling too much. Okay? Simple is best.

Financial Statements and Reports

Financial statements and other reports are your first, and primary, way to monitor various KPIs. If you choose to monitor on a monthly basis (which I recommend be your minimum frequency), then you probably want to check most of the following:

- Total Sales
- Total Cost of Goods Sold
- Gross Profit
- Total Expenses
- Net Profit
- Total Accounts Payable
- Total Accounts Receivable
- Aged Accounts Payable
- Aged Accounts Receivable
- Sales Tax Payable

Notice that none of the totals above tells you much on its own. The value of the data is not in a standalone number but in comparison to previous periods or to budget predictions. That's why tracking these numbers over time will give you increasingly more information.

For example, you might have a belief that Wednesday is your slowest day of business. But if you review what your POS system tells you, it might turn out that Tuesday is slow, but Wednesday has pretty decent sales spread out over the whole day. That kind of information can help you schedule staffing.

And if you track your Accounts Receivable, you might learn that over time there is a definite pattern to when customers pay. If you know when to expect your customer payments to come in, you can better plan paying your own bills.

In reviewing your financial statements, you might find that your Cost of Goods Sold for merchandise has been creeping up over the last year. That might indicate it's time to review your purchasing. Have you drifted to a slightly higher-cost supplier who comes in more frequently to see you? Is there a lower-cost supplier you've overlooked?

Depending on your business, you may or may not want to track all of the above, but you can track pieces inside each item. For instance, you might want to track your total sales by what you sold: services, products, or both. And with Cost of Goods Sold, you might want to track the costs for a single product. Tracking sales by item will tell you where to put your money and effort in terms of carrying inventory and marketing.

For example, if you own a day spa and sell both services and merchandise, you might notice some services sell less often than others. You might want to revamp some of the less popular ones into "add-on" services to see if that creates more interest. Or, if you put together "self-care kits" and some are not selling as well as others, you can review costs and sales and test whether individual products sell better outside the kits.

If your bookkeeping system is set up properly, your software will do most of this tracking for you. Good numbers equal instant tracking feedback. (And now you know why I wrote this book!) But don't overwhelm yourself with tracking too many items.

Ratios for Business Performance Evaluation

Along with tracking financial data like sales, costs, and profit, you can also evaluate business performance with quick calculations. Now it's time to get a little bit math-y again. Don't panic.

None of this is complicated math. We're just going to have a brief, painless discussion about ratios.

So, what's a ratio? A ratio is simply a means of expressing the relationship between two numbers via simple division. Basically, a fraction. (I know—I didn't like fractions in school either.) In this context, a ratio gives you a single number summary of a comparison between relevant, relational business financial numbers (after a brief, non-painful calculation). That is, ratios give you a way to measure various aspects of business performance.

For example, you can divide sales by the number of employees you have to find a value for "sales per employee." Monitoring that ratio might help you adjust staffing needs over periods of heavy, seasonal sales—you can see the point at which it becomes physically impossible for one person to sell more. Or maybe you learn that there is a point at which more labor does *not* increase sales.

There are several ratios you can consider using in monitoring your business performance. They fall into various categories—liquidity, leverage, efficiency, profitability—and each category has multiple ratios you can use. Some won't be valid for your business, but some will. If you have any nerd tendencies (you know, like me), you could build a simple spreadsheet for the ratios you want to track. Then if you fill in numbers from your financial statements every month, you could let the spreadsheet do the calculating.

I'll go over a few ratios from each category, and you can decide if you want to try using them. We'll use the financial statements from Doug's Premier Plumbing again, so here we go—back to the Balance Sheet!

Doug's Premier Plumbing, Inc.
Balance Sheet
As of October 31, 2018

	Oct 31, 2018
ASSETS	
Current Assets	
Checking/Savings	
Business Checking	35,457.19
Business Savings	500.00
Total Checking/Savings	35,957.19
Accounts Receivable	
Accounts Receivable	8,125.00
Total Accounts Receivable	8,125.00
Total Current Assets	44,082.19
Fixed Assets	
Computer & Office Equipment	2,500.00
Accumulated Depreciation	-846.12
Total Fixed Assets	1,653.88
TOTAL ASSETS	45,736.07
LIABILITIES & EQUITY	
Liabilities	
Current Liabilities	
Accounts Payable	2,317.29
Credit Cards	964.12
Payroll Liabilities	530.34
Line of Credit	4,569.28
Total Current Liabilities	8,381.03
Total Liabilities	8,381.03
Equity	
Owner Contributions	45,800.00
Owner Draws	-44,877.33
Total Owner Capital	922.67
Retained Earnings	9,054.28
Net Income	27,378.09
Total Equity	37,355.04
TOTAL LIABILITIES & EQUITY	45,736.07

Figure 27: Doug's Premier Plumbing Balance Sheet

Liquidity Ratios

Liquidity ratios are used to measure how easily your business can pay its obligations. Do you have enough cash or cash equivalents on hand to cover short-term debt? How many of your assets are "liquid"?

Liquidity ratios are some of the most basic business health-care checks you can track. Checking them is like checking your business blood pressure or blood glucose.

Current Ratio. The most basic liquidity ratio is the Current Ratio, which simply divides Current Assets by Current Liabilities. In this case Doug's Premier Plumbing has $44,082.19 in Current Assets and $8,381.03 in Current Liabilities, so his Current Ratio is 5.3.

$$\text{Current Ratio} = \frac{\text{Current Assets}}{\text{Current Liabilities}}$$

$$5.3 = \frac{44{,}082.19}{8{,}381.03}$$

Figure 28: Current Ratio Calculation for Doug's Premier Plumbing

What this tells us is that Doug's Premier Plumbing has over five times the cash and current assets on hand to cover what the company owes on a short-term basis. A good result here is anything over 1 (so Doug is in great shape!). If the result is less than 1, then your business has more current debt than current assets. That can be risky.

The Current Ratio includes Inventory in the Current Assets, so depending on your business, this ratio may be more useful, or less so. If you have a beauty salon that holds haircare products as inventory and has a steady stream of clients, you could probably have a sale and clear your shelves of products rather quickly if you needed to raise cash to pay bills. In other words, your inventory asset is easy to liquidate.

If, on the other hand, your inventory consists of high-cost items that you sell only a few times a year, your inventory is probably not going to be quick to liquidate should you need cash. As a result, the Current Ratio is less valuable to you. Instead, you probably want to use the Quick Ratio.

Quick Ratio. The Quick Ratio is nearly the same as the Current Ratio, but it first subtracts Inventory from Current Assets before dividing by Current Liabilities.

$$\text{Quick Ratio} = \frac{(\text{Current Assets - Inventory})}{\text{Current Liabilities}}$$

Figure 29: Quick Ratio Calculation

Since Doug's Premier Plumbing does not have inventory, I'm not showing a calculation here. But if you've got inventory on your books, you can see that a valid inventory number is important. As with the Current Ratio, ideally you want your Quick Ratio to be greater than 1.

Leverage Ratios

Leverage ratios represent how effectively your business is using debt. The use of credit is a natural part of doing business. I know, I know—"everyone" says debt is bad. But let's talk about that for a minute. If you do not use debt in business, you are limiting your purchasing power to *only* your cash on hand.

Here's an example: Doug's dad is a plumber (convenient, right?), and he is retiring and closing his business. He's offered to sell his last truck to Doug for $10,000. Doug wants another truck so he can take on more jobs, but he doesn't want to deplete his cash resources and he has heard "debt is bad," so he is hesitant.

But what if Doug looked first at how many more sales he could generate with an additional truck? If that truck lets Doug's crews get to more jobs, and as a result they can produce more revenue than the cost of the truck, then why not borrow the money to buy the truck? That's a simple example, but the point is that creating debt to create income is okay if it's done wisely and with some analysis.

Additionally, even if you haven't borrowed money, just the function of making sales and paying employees can create financial obligations. Remember, your current liabilities include Sales Tax Payable, Payroll Liabilities, Accounts Payable, and possibly more. Those are all considered short-term debt as they will be paid off in a year or less. Long-term debt is going to be paid down over more than a year.

In evaluating the amount of debt your business is carrying, two common measures are debt-to-assets and debt-to-equity.

Debt Ratio. The Debt Ratio (or Debt-to-Asset Ratio) measures the proportion of business assets funded with debt by dividing Total Liabilities by Total Assets. So again, "debt" refers to the liabilities, or money you owe to others, booked in the business. (See Figure 30 next page.)

A high ratio might indicate that assets have been acquired with debt, which is a higher risk if cash flow isn't sufficient to cover it. A low ratio might look good but also could mean that the business does not leverage debt to increase income, which means lower returns and income. A ratio of .4 or lower usually indicates manageable debt; that is, you are producing enough income and cash flow to service the debt. But it's difficult to specify an ideal ratio since industries vary and the context matters. If you have a small business that is in a leased space and you are looking at buying your own building, a lower ratio is going to be better. After you buy the building, your ratio is going to go up, and taking on more debt might push it too high.

$$\text{Debt Ratio} = \frac{\text{Total Liabilities}}{\text{Total Assets}}$$

$$0.18 = \frac{8{,}381.03}{45{,}736.07}$$

Figure 30: Debt Ratio Calculation for Doug's Premier Plumbing

Even if you did not borrow money to pay for your assets (equipment, vehicles, buildings, and so on), the debt ratio is how banks, lenders, and prospective buyers will evaluate the amount of debt your business is carrying.

Debt-to-Equity Ratio. The Debt-to-Equity Ratio measures how much of your business has been funded by you and how much has been funded by debt.

$$\text{Debt-to-Equity Ratio} = \frac{\text{Total Liabilities}}{\text{Total Equity}}$$

$$0.22 = \frac{8{,}381.03}{37{,}355.04}$$

Figure 31: Debt-to-Equity Calculation for Doug's Premier Plumbing

A high ratio might indicate a business underfunded by the owner; that is, using debt rather than owner contributions to fund assets. Using debt rather than owner contributions is not necessarily a bad thing, but something to consider if you are contemplating taking on more business debt or thinking about selling your business.

Efficiency Ratios

Efficiency ratios measure how effectively your business is functioning in areas such as turning over inventory or collecting Accounts Receivable.

Inventory Turnover Ratio. A manufacturing business will have inventory in several stages of processing: raw goods and materials, work in process, and finished goods. Efficiency ratios can be used to summarize how effectively your inventory is turning over or selling. Some manufacturing processes are quick (like food products) and some are slower (heavy equipment), but generally speaking, you do not want any inventory just sitting around. When inventory sits too long, it is considered obsolete—either outdated or too old to be used in manufacturing. When you cannot sell your inventory, you end up with wasted resources. Using inventory turnover ratios will help you track how effectively and efficiently you are using inventory to create sales.

The most common inventory efficiency ratio is Inventory Turnover. It is calculated by taking Cost of Goods Sold and dividing by Average Inventory. And Average Inventory can be calculated by adding the total of Beginning Inventory to the total of Ending Inventory for the month and dividing by two. What this tells you is how many times your inventory turned over in the month—in other words, how many times you sold and replaced your inventory. As you can imagine, turnover rates can vary wildly depending on your business and what you sell. If you have a high-traffic hair and nail salon with multiple stations rented, then your product sales are going to be small dollar amounts, but inventory turnover will be frequent. If you sell new cars, your sales will be large, but the inventory turnover is likely to be a lot less frequent.

A/R Turnover Ratio. Remember that when you sell products or services to someone and give them 15 or 30 days to pay you, you have extended credit to them. If they are slow to pay you, your income might look good with the sales recorded, but your cash flow is going to be hurtin' until you get paid. The A/R turnover ratio helps monitor how effectively you are collecting your Accounts Receivable.

The A/R Turnover Ratio is defined as Net Credit Sales divided by average Accounts Receivable for the period.

First, find your net credit sales total. This does not mean *credit card* sales; it means sales made on credit—that is, you are giving the customer time to pay (e.g., 30 days)—rather than paid on the spot. To calculate net credit sales, subtract any *cash* sales from your total sales for the period. In this sense, "cash" includes not only cash and checks but also debit and credit card payments. So if your August sales totaled $43,100 and several customers paid you on the spot with checks, cash or debit/credit cards totaling $5,610, then your credit sales are what's left when you subtract $5,610 from $43,100.

So Net Credit Sales = $43,100 – $5,610 = $37,490.

Then, calculate your *average* Accounts Receivable balance for the period. Average A/R is calculated by adding the beginning A/R balance to the ending A/R balance and dividing by two. So if your August Accounts Receivable balance was

$13,500 at the beginning of the month and $22,500 at the end of the month, the calculation is:

$$\$13{,}500 + \$22{,}500 = \$36{,}000 / 2 = \$18{,}000$$

That $18,000 is your average Accounts Receivable balance.

To calculate your Accounts Receivable turnover rate, divide the net credit sales by average A/R:

$$\frac{\text{(Total Sales - Cash Sales)}}{\text{(Beginning A/R Balance - Ending A/R Balance) / 2}} = \text{A/R Turnover Rate}$$

$$\frac{(43{,}100 - 5{,}610)}{(13{,}500 + 22{,}500) / 2} = 2.08$$

$$\frac{18{,}000}{37{,}490} = 2.08$$

Figure 32: Accounts Receivable Turnover Rate

What this tells us is that that A/R balances were cleared (paid!) just over twice in the month. A high rate of turnover means that customers are paying on time, and a low turnover rate could mean it's time to put more effort into collections. You need to decide how long you want to allow your customers to owe you money, and knowing your A/R Turnover Ratio may give you some idea where to start. Think about how frequently your suppliers ask you for payment, and then look at what kind of cash flow *in* you can expect from your customers. Alignment here means that you can better rely on incoming funds to pay your own suppliers and vendors.

Profitability Ratios

Now we are moving to the Profit & Loss statement to look at profitability ratios, which, as you might guess, assess . . . profitability! Or rather, they assess how efficient your business is at generating income from operations. You are spending money and effort to produce income, so profitability ratios are designed to measure how efficiently you do that. Doug's full P&L is on the next page for reference.

Gross Profit Margin. Recall that Gross Profit is how much you have left over to cover operating expenses after you subtract the cost of sales (COGS) from your Revenue (Total Income in QuickBooks). Gross Profit Margin expresses the amount remaining as a percentage of that Revenue and is calculated by taking the Gross Profit and dividing by Revenue. (Sometimes it is described as Gross Profit divided by Sales; Sales is another term that can replace Total Income as you look at the QuickBooks image in the next few figures.)

To find the Gross Profit Margin for Doug's Premier Plumbing, we are going to use Total Income (aka Gross Income or Revenue) and Total COGS.

Doug's Premier Plumbing, Inc.
Profit & Loss
As of October 31, 2018

	Jan 1 - Oct 31, 2018
Ordinary Income/Expense	
Residential Services	49,238.75
Commercial Services	35,249.22
Total Income	84,487.97
Cost of Goods Sold	
Parts and Materials	16,238.56
Subcontractor Costs	10,175.00
Total COGS	26,413.56
Gross Profit	58,074.41

Figure 33: Gross Profit Margin Numbers on Profit & Loss

Doug's Premier Plumbing, Inc.
Profit & Loss
As of October 31, 2018

	Jan 1 - Oct 31, 2018
Ordinary Income/Expense	
Residential Services	49,238.75
Commercial Services	35,249.22
Total Income	84,487.97
Cost of Goods Sold	
Parts and Materials	16,238.56
Subcontractor Costs	10,175.00
Total COGS	26,413.56
Gross Profit	58,074.41
Expense	
Advertising Expense	450.00
Business License & Fees	75.00
Car/Truck Expense	1,223.17
Charitable Contributions	150.00
Depreciation Expense	846.12
Dues and Subscriptions	175.00
Insurance	4,150.00
Maintenance/Janitorial	1,641.25
Meals, Local	178.25
Office Expenses	1,075.00
Postage and Delivery	0.00
Professional Fees	119.53
Legal Fees	600.00
Accounting Fees	2,319.00
Total Professional Fees	3,038.53
Rent	7,005.00
Repairs and Maintenance	390.00
Telephone	895.24
Payroll Expenses	
Wages	6,576.00
Payroll Tax Expense	2,326.17
Total Payroll Expenses	8,902.17
Utilities	501.59
Total Expense	30,696.32
Net Ordinary Income	27,378.09
Net Income	**27,378.09**

Figure 34: Doug's Premier Plumbing P&L

We first subtract Total COGS from Total Income to get Gross Profit, and then we divide Gross Profit by Total Income. So Doug's Gross Profit Margin equals ($84,487.97 minus $26,413.56) divided by $84,487.97. The arithmetic leads us to a ratio of 0.6873, or 68.7%.

$$\text{Gross Profit Margin} = \frac{(\text{Total Income} - \text{Cost of Goods Sold})}{\text{Total Income}}$$

$$68.7\% = \frac{(84{,}487.97 - 26{,}413.56)}{84{,}487.97}$$

Figure 35: Doug's Gross Profit Margin

So what does that tell Doug exactly? It tells him that 68.7% of his revenue is left over after direct product and sales costs. This ratio is your first stop in knowing whether you are making sales that cover your basic costs for products or materials, and whether your sales prices are high enough. If you sell products or services that you either build or buy, then you have to know your margins.

Gross Profit Margin is a very informative ratio, and one every business owner should understand. If you create gift baskets, for example, you can calculate your gross profit margin on every basket, *even before you create it*, simply by knowing the costs for each item you use to build the baskets. Considering different sales prices can help you decide what kind of margin you need for each. And if you have a salon and want to sell a new line of products, you can estimate your sales price by adding your desired margin to the cost of each product.

Net Profit Margin. Net Profit Margin gives you a percentage of what is left in profit after all your expenses are recorded. It is calculated by dividing Net Income by Total Income (remember that Net Income and Total Income might be called something else depending on your software or who you are talking to) and then multiplying by 100 to get a percentage.

So for Doug's Premier Plumbing . . .

$$\text{Net Profit Margin} = \frac{\text{Net Income}}{\text{Total Income}}$$

$$0.32 = \frac{27{,}378.09}{84{,}487.97}$$

Figure 36: Doug's Net Profit Margin

If you multiply 0.32 by 100 you get 32%. That means that after all his expenses, Doug has 32% of his total sales left.

Net Profit Margin is not something you want to just check once a year—that won't give you any comparative information value. Tracking it monthly will show you how it changes throughout the year based on the flow of revenue and expenses through your business.

For example, a corner grocery store might not experience much variation in monthly sales, but a golf club in Alaska is likely to experience a drop in monthly income when the weather gets cold. Your business sales and expenses can be affected by season, staffing, supply, demand, and more. If your sales revenue goes up, but your expenses increase faster, then your Net Profit Margin is going to reflect that (by going down).

Ratios like Net Profit Margin give you a single percentage summary that is easy to compare month-to-month. There are a lot of other ratios you can use to track different segments and functions of your business, but I just wanted to give you a few. And I should probably give you a round of applause for reading this far! Yay, you!

Chapter Summary

As a small business owner, it's easy to get sucked into the daily operations and end up with your nose buried in the details. Doing a monthly review of key performance indicators (KPIs) gives you a chance to step back and take a wide-angle look at your business.

There are some common KPIs across businesses, but others are industry-specific, so you need to consider which will mean the most to you and your business. Your KPIs may include numbers from your financial statements, calculated ratios, or sales or other performance standards.

Ratios condense your financial statement numbers into single measures for tracking ease and comparison over time. Leverage ratios measure liquidity (the ability to pay off current debt), how effectively you are using debt to fund business activities, and the ownership split between you and your creditors if you are paying off long-term debt. Efficiency ratios measure how effectively you are using business resources to generate revenue. Profitability ratios tell you how well you are controlling costs and making sales.

Keep your KPIs as simple as possible to avoid overwhelming yourself with data, but do track what will be meaningful to you.

Ideally give your business a checkup as you finish reviewing the month, but at minimum review KPIs every quarter-end and year-end.

9

Going Forward with the Lights On

This is the final chapter (Whew!), and I want to give you some ideas for moving forward. Your business will change over time—sometimes within a short time frame and sometimes over a long period. As a rock star business owner, you need to monitor the changes, be aware of the influences that drive the changes, and make strategic decisions that keep your business responsive and adaptable.

Some of the challenges will include maintaining staffing, watching and adapting to trends and cycles, avoiding complacency, and continually monitoring internal and external conditions. And one key change may be in yourself.

Let's talk briefly about how you can monitor changes and respond to them.

Find Help!

As an entrepreneur you know you cannot do everything, but it is still natural to try. Don't! Get help. What kind of help you need will depend on the kind of business you have, the flow of sales, cash, and data through your workplace, and what you want to do with your business.

Bookkeeper. As I said at the beginning of this book, my first recommendation is that you get a good bookkeeper. That doesn't mean hiring a full-time employee necessarily; it could be a part-time contract bookkeeper, someone who comes in one a week or once a month. And I hate to say it, but there are some bad bookkeepers out there (as with any industry, you find some good employees and some big-time duds). Unfortunately, a bad bookkeeper can also create the risk of embezzlement, liability over unpaid payroll taxes, and other messy situations.

I could write a separate book on screening and hiring the right bookkeeper, but instead I'll summarize my thoughts here. Do some research. Ask your CPA for referrals. Go to the websites for QuickBooks or Xero to find certified advisors. And do not hesitate to fire a bookkeeper who will not give you good information to help run your business.

Tax Professional. Besides a good bookkeeper, you should have a good tax professional. If you pay taxes every year—and presumably if you're reading this book, you do—then work with a CPA or tax pro to manage your taxable income. They know things you and I do not know about how to reduce your tax liability, manage tax payments throughout the year, and manage audit risk.

If you take your business and/or personal books to a tax pro once a year to have your annual federal and other tax returns filed, don't expect them to dig through your transactions and make suggestions. CPA firms are insanely busy during tax season. They do not voluntarily add hours or charges to your bill just to take a ramble through your business books. You won't get helpful tips, in-depth corrections, or guidance. They are going to make as few adjustments as necessary to make sure your tax returns are filed. Then they rush off to work on the next tax return in the monster pile on their desk.

If you feel like you need some help with managing your financial data to produce a lower tax bill, make an appointment *after* tax season. Ask for a consultation and go in with a list of specific concerns and questions. Looking at the bottom line of your tax return means backing up and looking at each component that lands on it. This is where your CPA or tax pro should excel at helping you, but you need to ask specifically for that kind of help.

I've worked with one client who has multiple businesses, all taxed on his personal tax return. He and I met with his CPA after tax season one year to find out what kind of changes he needed to make. He reminded us that it was an optimal time for the owner to purchase a new truck—which he was happy to do. We also learned that he needed to put himself on the payroll with both companies.

Other Professionals. Beyond bookkeeping and taxes, there are other business support professionals out there. The kind of help you ask for will depend on what element of your business you feel is struggling. You can find all kinds of help with inventory management, Accounts Receivable collections, writing, marketing and social media, human resources, payroll processing, web design and maintenance, and more. You can also consider working with a mentor through the U.S. Small Business Administration's recommended SCORE program (score.org).

Systems. Are your processes and systems working efficiently and effectively for you? Think about the systems you are already using, such as a point-of-sale system or inventory tracking system. Computer-based systems like these will make your bookkeeping more efficient. Also consider how you can reduce the amount of transition time as paper documents move through your business.

It used to be that you were limited by geography when seeking help with your business. Now as the world shrinks through online access to people and information, you can find training, resources, guides, and more. You just have to start looking.

Look Back before Moving Forward

Growing a business does not just mean increasing sales. You must have a fully functional business system, or you will burn yourself out or, worse, cripple your business.

What part of your business would be most likely to break down first under pressure?

When you feel ready to move your business forward, turn around and look back inside your business first. I recommend taking your business apart (mentally, of course!) into the following segments and reviewing each one before actively pursuing growth.

Foundation. Your foundation includes your business structure (e.g., sole proprietor, LLC), insurance, licenses, and so on. Have you outgrown anything, including insurance levels or business structure? If you want to grow your business, you need a solid foundation to build on.

Customers/Clients. Do you know who represents your target market? When you step back after several years in business, has your market shifted? Look at who represents most of your customer/client base, and see what they need. Are you missing a market segment on which you could focus some advertising dollars and increase sales? If you are starting a new business, how can you most effectively direct advertising to the customers/clients you want to attract?

Products/Services. Review your sales and services. What's selling? What isn't selling? Remember the profit margin discussion last chapter? Pretend you are a consultant and assess your product/service mix. What needs to change?

Presence. Your presence includes your physical location—your building, parking lot, warehouse—as well as your business presence as a whole—your website, social media, branding. How can you strengthen it or build it up? Parking lot ready for repaving? Social media presence too inactive, inconsistent, or random? You want to look like a strong, successful entity, so clean up, spiff up, and refresh all aspects of your location whenever they start to get worn.

Suppliers/Vendors. You rely on other people for products you resell or to provide a service to you in support of your business. If a supplier closes, do you have alternatives? Are your product costs high? Are there other lower-cost options out there? What is your vendor selection process? How well is it working?

Employees/Contractors. Staffing always presents challenges. One bad employee can infect the good ones, and good employees need to be rewarded. What can you do to keep the good employees, and how can you find better people to replace your duds? How well are you paying attention to job market shifts? Are you keeping up with market rates and best practices? Is it time for better human resources policies and procedures?

Finances. Finances—all the transaction recording, reporting, loan repayment, and on and on—is probably the first segment most business owners naturally drift to for review, but it's also probably the least likely to need immediate change. No, seriously, think about it: all of the previous segments we just went through are what drive costs and revenue. When you change, fix, or repair those, then the financial segment will inevitably change. So what I'd like you to do with *this* segment is not to think about how to improve the numbers but rather to think about how to improve your financial *management*. Do you need to upgrade or add inventory control software? Hire a new bookkeeper? Hire a virtual Chief Financial Officer so you can get assistance with monthly or quarterly reviews? Visit your tax pro for guidance?

Future Planning. What does your business need going forward? What are your goals for your business? Do you want to sell it someday to help fund your retirement? Are you going to hand it off to an heir to run while you retire? Think about what your goals are and how you can start supporting those goals right now.

You. Yup, you are the last segment we are going to review. As the business owner, you are both the driving force and the built-in limitation to your business. Are you going strong, or do you need help or training? How can you best support yourself in becoming both a strong leader and a skilled manager?

When you break your business apart into segments, you can evaluate them individually and think about change and growth in smaller chunks. And then you can put the chunks back together to evaluate them collectively.

And that flows into the next section . . .

Do a SWOT Analysis

Once you review your business by each of the eight components above, you can do what is called a SWOT analysis.

If you have not yet come across a SWOT analysis in your business life, hold on, 'cause I'm about to teach you a cool tool.

SWOT is an acronym for Strengths, Weaknesses, Opportunities, and Threats. This is an excellent business tool that's been around for years. It looks at both internal and external factors and puts them in the context of how they affect your business positively or negatively.

- Strengths and Weaknesses are *internal* factors that help or hinder you (respectively) in achieving your goals.
- Opportunities and Threats are *external* factors that help or hinder you (respectively) in achieving your goals.

Once you have an understanding of these factors, you can prioritize actions to take to improve your position in achieving your goals. We'll go through a sample SWOT analysis to show you how it works and what it might look like on a small scale.

To do a SWOT, I suggest using a flip chart, but you can write on a piece of paper or type up your notes too. You will want to be able to refer back to your SWOT over time as you update it—do you see positive shifts based on the changes you are making?

I'd also suggest you have key staff (at least one other person) work through these with you in order to brainstorm more comprehensive results. We've all heard that two brains are better than one, but that might depend on the other brain. Ask someone you trust, but also someone who understands how businesses work.

So let's go back to Doug's Premier Plumbing again. Here is what Doug and his COO, Jan, listed on their SWOT.

Strengths (internal factors that help achieve goals):

- Strong branding that is visible on all vehicles
- Licensed for both commercial and residential work
- Insurance is more than adequate for growth of up to three additional trucks
- Two strong employees who work well and represent the company well

Weaknesses (internal factors that hinder goals):

- The current formation is a sole proprietorship; CPA recommends changing to an LLC (Limited Liability Company) to protect personal assets
- The balance on current liabilities is high, putting the business at risk if sales drop due to competition
- Having trouble hiring an additional person
- No HR policies in place; hiring has been okay so far

Opportunities (external factors that could help achieve goals):

- Changing to an LLC would make the business look more professional and might increase bid opportunities
- Rumor has it a competitor is going out of business. Can we increase visibility anywhere to gain more market share? Will there be qualified people who need jobs?

Threats (external factors that can hinder goals):

- Relatively low start-up cost means someone else could come along and create competition
- The number of other plumbing companies in the area creates a very competitive market; mistakes or bad service could make customer retention difficult
- A new company could hire the two good employees away from Doug with better offers

Note that it is possible for the same factor to be both a positive and a potential negative. For example, if one of your business strengths is the two guys on your payroll, it could also be a considerable threat if another competing business can hire them away from you.

Be as comprehensive as you can in listing factors—you might end up with a lot! So then go through and score each element by how critical it is. You can use something simple like high, medium, low.

Can you see how that sort of ranking might go with our Doug example? (If you went through and scored each item for how critical it might be, give yourself a gold star.)

Now that you have a SWOT analysis, it's time to do something with it: it's time for action items. When you look at each of your strengths, weaknesses, opportunities, and threats, did anything come up that you need to do?

Using our example, Doug's top priorities might be to:

- Change the business formation to an LLC,
- Review and update hiring and HR policies, and
- Review his employees' wages and benefits.

Stay competitive, my friend!

Watch for Trends and Cycles

Once you are doing regular financial and business reviews, you will begin to see the impact of trends and cycles. Most of the time, when the subject of trends and cycles comes up, someone is talking about economics on a national or global level and how trends and cycles affect small business in general. I want you to scale that back and start looking for trends and cycles within your business. Sales go up, sales go down. Costs go up, costs go down. Nothing is static in business. It might appear to be, but when you back away and look at the big picture, you'll see different patterns.

Trends. Let's talk about trends first. (And we're not talking about high-waist, acid-wash jeans making a second or third comeback to the fashion scene.) A trend, in terms of your small business, is an incremental movement over time. If your revenue goes up by 9% every year despite ups and downs over individual months, you are seeing a trend. If your product costs increase by 9% every year, you are seeing a trend. (See how recognizing that trend makes creating a budget easier?) You might see trends that develop over the span of a year, such as one product beginning to outsell other products, or a product that gradually drops in sales every month. You see these patterns through the accurate recording of data (back to that again!).

When you see a trend, you should ask yourself why it is there. What's driving it?

Let's say Doug's Premier Plumbing sees revenue from new residential services going up, while emergency call-outs are going down. This could be an easy trend to explain if, for example, Doug made a strategic decision to start doing more residential plumbing for developers rather than house calls on existing structures.

However, what if that's not the case? Has the staff at Doug's Premier Plumbing become less responsive to emergency call-outs? Are existing customers starting to go to a competitor?

And what happens if new construction slows? Then Doug might want that call-out service back, so what does he need to do to hang onto it and keep those customers happy?

Monitoring trends allows you to respond by managing staffing, adapting business hours, adding services, or even dropping a pre-packaged service that's no longer cost-effective.

Cycles. While trends show movement in one direction, cycles ebb and flow. The numbers predictably move up and down. Cycles move in patterns that might be economically driven, seasonally driven, or even driven by an academic calendar if your labor force or customer base is enrolled in school. For example, if you own a coffee shop on or near a college campus, you might see a predictable cycle in revenue dropping over the summer. Or if you are a mobile locksmith, you might see an increase in business with new apartment move-ins right before school starts. Anyone with a retail business that experiences a holiday rush knows firsthand what a seasonal cycle looks like. Not all cycles are as dramatic as a Black Friday holiday crush, but if you start watching in your own business, you may see some.

In tracking cycles, you can look at when your highest and lowest sales fall in the month, what your busiest and slowest times of the year are, and whether the wave of new construction hitting your region is something that you want to begin bidding on. Cycles can give you feedback on when to reorder supplies, when to schedule open hours, and how to staff to accommodate heavier call volume.

Relative to your business, think of trends as something to which you need to respond to control the impact on your business. And think of cycles as something that you can manage around. That's a simplification, but that's the essence of how trends and cycles apply to your business. And knowing what you are watching gives you the power to adapt, flex, or change to best manage it.

Plan to Succeed

Planning for success is a simple concept that a lot of business owners overlook. I see how easy it is to get caught up in the daily details of being invested in your business. But planning for success is critical.

Set Goals. Decide what you want to accomplish each year and each quarter. Set your sales goal for the year. Define what kind of reach you want to have on social media. Set performance metrics that will help keep customers happy. Set goals that are attainable and realistic to your business and to the economy in which you are working.

Develop Structure. If your business is such that you can organize your tasks in time chunks or blocks, define your workweek in a way that supports what you need to get done. For example, I use daily themes. I use Mondays for blogging, social media, and my own bookkeeping. Tuesdays, Thursdays, and Fridays are for client work and/or meetings. And Wednesdays I set aside for working on continuing education, whether for certifications or for my own knowledge.

Set Boundaries. Your time is valuable, and there are certain tasks only you can do; other tasks can be delegated. In order to protect your valuable time, you may need to set boundaries. For example, if you have young employees, you might end up having to train them how to be employees—show up on time, stay off your phone while you're working, and so on. Customers might also expect to deal with you as the business owner, rather than with a staff member. You have to "teach" the people you interact with that you must have time to do other tasks to keep your business stable and profitable. Set some boundaries, and be conscious of when and where you decide to flex them.

Check In with Yourself. Schedule a monthly or quarterly check-in meeting with yourself. Give yourself a list of what to review, and work through the following questions:

- What is working well in my business? Think in terms of the same nine segments we discussed earlier: foundation, customers/clients, products/services, presence, suppliers/vendors, employees/contractors, finances, growth and development plans, and yourself.
- What needs help from me? What can I delegate or drop?
- How are my financials? Compare this year to last year, this quarter to last quarter, this month to last month.
- Am I on track with my goals? If so, is there anything that could derail me? If not, how can I get back on track? And were my goals realistic?

Treat the meeting with yourself like an appointment with your favorite client. Go somewhere you won't be interrupted, and work through a good review with coffee (or wine!).

Get Support. If you feel isolated or alone as a business owner, consider joining a mastermind group. That will put you with peers you can relate to and get encouragement from. Support and accountability go a long way toward reaching goals.

Don't Get Complacent

One other thing I want to discuss about moving forward successfully in your business is complacency. Complacency is a death sentence for businesses. If you assume that nothing has changed, nothing is going to change, and you do not need to monitor your market (external environment) or your operations (internal environment), you might be putting your business at risk.

Please, please, please do not fall into a pattern of complacency. Do a monthly review. Work through a SWOT analysis for your business. Heck, do a SWOT analysis for your competitors! What might you learn? Keep monitoring the local economy, the flow of potential customers, your existing customers, and anything else that can affect your business.

If a larger neighboring business closes, will it affect traffic to YOUR business? I have watched the local mall lose anchor stores recently, and I can't help but wonder how it will affect the smaller retailers.

One business owner I know created a sale specifically for active military personnel when he heard that a competitor had fired members of the military who had gotten orders that transferred them away from their off-base jobs. Keeping his ear to the ground gave this business owner a chance to offer a discounted product and promote it positively.

Keep your attention tuned both inward and outward as you work in and on your business. Expecting change will allow you to jump on opportunities when they come up as well as respond when something goes sideways.

One Final Thing: Succession Planning

This may not be a fun thing to talk about, but as a responsible business owner you need to give some thought to a succession plan. A succession plan is like a guardianship plan for your business. If something happens to you, what do you want to happen to your business? If you get sick and cannot work, who will fill in for you? Or worse, if you pass away, what do you want to see done? There are a variety of ways to handle a succession plan, but it is NOT something you should just scribble down on a napkin over a Philly cheesesteak.

Talk to an attorney and your CPA; plan for this eventuality. Talk about it with your loved ones. I want to be clear: the only way to do this right is with professional legal and tax advice. You are working hard to build, grow, or sustain your business, so give it a future after you are gone.

Chapter Summary

Do not think you have to do this business-owner thing alone or without help. Consider what kind of help you need. Get a good bookkeeper, and work with a good CPA to not only file your tax returns but to assist you mid-year in planning for taxes.

Use tools like the SWOT analysis to review your business's strengths, weaknesses, opportunities, and threats. Look internally and externally for the areas that need your attention or that you can capitalize on to increase your market share.

Learn to notice trends and cycles in your business. This will help you get better at managing cash flow, scheduling staff, and stocking inventory.

Plan for success, and do not allow yourself to fall into complacency. Don't assume that one really good financial year will mean every year will be like that. Take care of your business and when you are ready to sell it and retire, it will take care of you.

Glossary

Account numbers – Optional index numbering system that is part of most accounting software. Mostly useful for a chart of accounts that is extensive.

Accounting – The process and function of applying and using skills and knowledge to review, analyze, and interpret bookkeeping data. It is the progressive step beyond bookkeeping to make use of the numbers, and it might also include the bookkeeping.

Accounting equation – Assets = Liabilities + Equity. This is the formula that shows up on the Balance Sheet.

Accounts Payable (A/P) – Bills that are entered into your accounting system that you have not yet paid but will pay by the due dates.

Accounts Payable aging report – A report that sorts out and lists what you owe to others by the due date.

Accounts Receivable (A/R) – The money owed to you on invoices you have sent to your customers but they have not yet paid.

Accounts Receivable aging report – A report that sorts out and lists what others owe to you by the due dates.

Accounts Receivable turnover ratio – A measure of how frequently your business collects amounts owed by customers.

Accrual accounting – A method of accounting that records transactions for revenue and expenses when the transaction is created, not when the funds are received or paid. You can use accrual accounting or cash accounting, but not both.

Asset – Something of value that your business owns that is essential to operations. Assets might include land, buildings, furniture, fixtures, equipment, vehicles, and more.

Automated clearing house (ACH) transfer – An electronic form of payment that is batched together with other payments at the bank and sent to the recipient of the funds within one to two days.

Average Accounts Receivable – Calculated by adding the beginning Accounts Receivable balance and the ending Accounts Receivable balance and dividing by 2.

Balance Sheet – The financial statement that lists asset, liability, and equity account balances. It is the sum of your business in a snapshot, and all the account totals roll forward each period.

Bank feed – The transaction downloads that come directly into your accounting software from your bank account. A feed helps automate data entry, but it is not complete until recorded.

Bills – Amounts your business owes, which might include utilities, supplies and materials, and other expenses.

Bookkeeping – The process and function of systematically recording business transactions according to standardized guidelines. It generally does not include the accounting function of data interpretation and adjusting.

Bookkeeping consistency – Recording transactions by the same dates, names, and purposes over the life of your business.

Business legal structure – Legal categorization of your business entity as recognized by local, regional, and governmental authorities; might include sole proprietorship, LLC, C-Corp, and so on.

Cash accounting – A method of bookkeeping and accounting that recognizes income and expenses only when income is actually received and when expenses are actually paid. You can use cash accounting or accrual accounting, but not both.

Cash flow – The flow of cash and cash equivalents through your business; ideally you have enough cash (or equivalents) coming into your business to pay your obligations, regardless of whether you are making a profit.

Chart of Accounts – The standard index of accounting categories to which you record your transactions.

Cost of Goods Sold (COGS) – A category of accounts that includes the direct costs of making a sale: materials used, labor used, credit card fees, and so on.

Credit – The right side of a two-sided accounting entry.

Current ratio – A measure of how easily your company can pay off its current obligations.

Cycles – A predictable and expected change in income and expenses in your business; a cycle could cover a month, a quarter, a year, or several years.

Debit – The left side of a two-sided accounting entry.

Debt ratio – A measure of the proportion of a company's assets funded by debt; calculated by dividing Total Liabilities by Total Assets.

Debt-to-equity ratio – A measure of how much of your company's equity was funded by you and how much funded by debt; calculated by dividing Total Liabilities by Total Equity.

Double-entry accounting/bookkeeping – An accounting system that requires two sides to every entry: an action (paying a bill, writing a check, using a debit card) and a definition (the purpose of the transaction).

Efficiency ratios – Several calculations that measure how efficiently your business is using assets to manage liabilities.

Electronic funds transfer (EFT) – A classification of payment types that includes ACH, mobile payment platforms, wire transfers, direct deposit, and credit or debit card payments.

Equity – This represents ownership of the company; a group of accounts on the Balance Sheet that sums up life-to-date ownership activities.

Expenses – Expenditures that are necessary to operations and are recorded to reduce the taxable income of the business.

Financial statements – There are three financial statements: a Balance Sheet and a Profit & Loss Statement that together sum up a business's financial operations, and a Statement of Cash Flows that explains cash changes.

Generally accepted accounting principles (GAAP) – A set of standards for recording and reporting business transactions.

Gross Profit – The first level of business profit after deducting the cost of sales; calculated Total Income minus Cost of Goods Sold.

Gross Profit Margin – The percentage of sales left over after COGS is deducted; calculated (Total Income minus COGS) divided by Total Income and multiplied by 100.

Income – Refers to Revenue or Sales, but for clarity the term should be prefaced by "gross" or "net."

Income Statement – The detailed report that summarizes revenue and expenses for the report period; also called Profit & Loss Statement, or P&L.

Inventory turnover ratio – The number of times inventory has been bought and sold in a period.

Invoice – A document sent to a customer that tells them how much they owe you.

Journal entry – A means of making an accounting entry for transactions that were made outside of your business or for accounting adjustments or corrections; generally done by a knowledgeable bookkeeper or tax pro.

Key performance indicators (KPIs) – Business performance measures, expressed either in numbers or percentages, that are tracked over time.

Leverage ratios – Several measures of how a business's debt compares to either assets or equity and indicate measures of risk; if the leverage ratio is too high, a business may not be able to service its debts; if the ratio is too low, a business may not using debt effectively to grow.

Liability – What the business owes to others, including Accounts Payable, payroll, liabilities for taxes, or loans.

Liquid assets – Business assets that can be easily converted to cash at a minimal loss in value to pay financial responsibilities; may include actual cash, inventory that is easy to sell, certificates of deposit, bonds, or other money market investments.

Liquidity ratios – Several measures that assess how easily a business can pay off its obligations.

Month-end close – An accounting process that records a date through which numbers have been approved; a password may be used to prevent accidental changes to prior periods.

Net credit sales – Sales made on credit and owed to you by your customers; calculated by subtracting Cash Sales from Total Sales.

Net Income – The bottom line on the Profit & Loss Statement; calculated from Total Income minus COGS minus Expenses; also called Net Profit (or Net Loss).

Net Profit (or Net Loss) – The bottom line on the Profit & Loss Statement; calculated Total Income minus COGS minus Expenses; also called Net Income.

Net Profit Margin – The percentage of income left after COGS and all expenses have been deducted; calculated by dividing Net Income by Total Income.

Operating capital – Cash used to support daily operations.

Owner contribution/distribution – Money that a business owner has put in or withdrawn from a business.

Point-of-sale (POS) system – Centralized software and hardware for completing sales transactions; may also include inventory management.

Profit & Loss statement (P&L) – The report that summarizes revenue and expenses for the period; also called Income Statement.

Profitability ratios – Several measures that assess how well a business generates a profit from business activities.

Quick ratio – A measure of how easily a business can cover its obligations with available cash. It does not include inventory or other non-cash assets.

Ratio – A measure showing the relationship between two amounts, generally how many times one number must be multiplied to equal the other.

Reclassify/reclass – Making an accounting entry that moves an amount from one account to another for clarification or corrective purposes.

Reconciliation – The bookkeeping process that matches third-party information (bank statements, credit card statements, loan statements, etc.) to your business books and makes any necessary corrections.

Retained Earnings – An account in the Equity section of the Balance Sheet that shows a cumulative life-to-date summary of profit and loss. It is calculated automatically, so do not make manual changes to this account; only a qualified bookkeeper or tax pro should record changes to this account.

Revenue – What your business has earned through business activities before any deductions are made; also called Total Income or Total Sales.

Sales tax payable – The amount collected with sales and recorded as owed to various tax authorities.

Start-up capital – The funding used for starting a business; might be acquired through loans or savings.

Statement of Cash Flows – A financial statement that reconciles Net Income to changes in cash and cash equivalents to show cash left on hand.

Succession plan – A business plan that defines who will take over for you when you leave the business for any reason.

SWOT analysis – A business planning tool that assesses business Strengths, Weaknesses, Opportunities, and Threats.

Tax planning – A business review with a tax professional before year-end, with enough time to make critical changes if necessary.

Tax preparation – The process of calculating and filing a tax return for your business based on your recorded information.

Total Income – What your business has earned through business activities before any deductions are made; also called Revenue or Total Sales.

Total Sales – What your business has earned through business activities before any deductions are made; also called Revenue or Total Income.

Transaction dates – The date by which business transactions are recorded; rules for transaction dates vary for cash accounting and accrual accounting.

Trend – A pattern over time that shows an increase or decrease in some business measure, e.g., decreasing sales of a particular product, increasing profit margin.

Use tax – Self-reported tax on items purchased for use in your business on which you were not charged sales tax.

Resources

There are a lot of resources out there for business owners, and I'm only listing a few of them here, but these are some of my go-tos.

American Institute of Certified Public Accountants (AICPA, https://www.aicpa.org). While the AICPA is a membership association for CPAs, its website also offers valuable information to the public, including financial literacy resources as well as help finding a CPA.

LegalZoom (https://www.legalzoom.com). If you want to get more information on business formation or other business concerns (copyrights, patents, or trademarks), LegalZoom is a good place to start.

QuickBooks (https://www.quickbooks.com). There are multiple versions of QuickBooks bookkeeping software available, including both cloud-based and desktop, and you can find comparisons here. Or you can work your way further into the website to https://quickbooks.intuit.com/r/ and check out resources for business owners. You can also use the search function to find a QuickBooks Pro Advisor to work with you on your business at https://quickbooks.intuit.com/find-an-accountant/.

Xero (https://www.xero.com/us). Xero is an online alternative to QuickBooks. It has a simple pricing structure, and you can find a Xero advisor from the same webpage.

FreshBooks (https://www.freshbooks.com/). FreshBooks is cloud-based accounting software that is ideal for a solopreneur who does not own business assets and wants an easy structure for invoicing clients.

Small Business Administration (SBA, https://www.sba.gov). The SBA offers a TON of information, including guides on planning, starting, managing, and growing a business. The SBA also has online courses you can take, and there are links to connect with business mentors through SCORE, a program in which retired executives volunteer to help new business owners.

Me! Connect with me online at www.benchmark-business-services.com. There, you'll find my blog as well as free e-books and guides, and there's a Contact Me form if you have specific questions. You can also find me on Facebook as Benchmark Business Services (@bbs2009) or on Instagram as @lesliemenard.

About the Author

LESLIE MENARD is a business consultant, strategist, and contract bookkeeper in the state of Washington. She has been working in the accounting profession for longer than she will admit. She has earned a BS in Business Communications, an MA in Organizational Leadership, and an MS in Human Resources.

Find Leslie online at benchmark-business-services.com, on Facebook (@bbs2009), and on Instagram (@lesliemenard).

Made in the USA
Monee, IL
08 November 2026

68012207R00100